ISBN 978-1-5280-3983-3
PIBN 10914521

For support please visit www.forgottenbooks.com

1 MONTH OF
FREE
READING

at
www.ForgottenBooks.com

By purchasing this book you are eligible for one month membership to ForgottenBooks.com, giving you unlimited access to our entire collection of over 1,000,000 titles via our web site and mobile apps.

To claim your free month visit:

www.forgottenbooks.com/free914521

English
Français
Deutsche
Italiano
Español
Português

www.forgottenbooks.com

Mythology Photography **Fiction**
Fishing Christianity **Art** Cooking
Essays Buddhism Freemasonry
Medicine **Biology** Music **Ancient
Egypt** Evolution Carpentry Physics
Dance Geology **Mathematics** Fitness
Shakespeare **Folklore** Yoga Marketing
Confidence Immortality Biographies
Poetry **Psychology** Witchcraft
Electronics Chemistry History **Law**
Accounting **Philosophy** Anthropology
Alchemy Drama Quantum Mechanics
Atheism Sexual Health **Ancient History**
Entrepreneurship Languages Sport
Paleontology Needlework Islam
Metaphysics Investment Archaeology
Parenting Statistics Criminology
Motivational

NORTHWESTERN UNIVERSITY

COLLEGE OF LIBERAL A

EVANSTON, ILL.

CIRCULAR OF INFORMATION

1897-98.

NORTHWESTERN UNIVERSITY

COLLEGE OF LIBERAL ARTS

EVANSTON, ILL.

Special attention is called to the fact that the college year is now divided into semesters, the first semester closing February 9, and the second semester beginning February 10, 1897.

Examinations for admission are held on September 20 and 21, 1897, and college work begins September 23, 1897.

ANNOUNCEMENTS FOR 1897-98.

September 20 and 21, Monday and Tuesday, Examination for Admission to College of Liberal Arts.

September 23, Thursday, **First Semester Begins.**

September 23, Thursday, Supplementary Examinations.

October 6, Wednesday, Cleveland Prize Contestants Announced.

November 24, Wednesday Evening, to November 29, Monday Morning, Thanksgiving Recess.

December 22, Wednesday Evening, to January 2, 1898, Sunday Evening, Holiday Recess.

1898.

January 11, Tuesday, Appointment of Gage Prize Contestants.

January 14, Friday, Cleveland Prize Contest.

January 27, Thursday, Day of Prayer for Colleges.

February 1, Tuesday, to February 8, Tuesday, Regular Examinations.

February 9, Wednesday, Additional Examinations.

February 9, Wednesday Evening, to February 14, Monday Morning, Mid-Year Recess.

February 10, Thursday, **Second Semester Begins.**

February 14, Monday, Supplementary Examinations.

April 1, Thursday Evening, to April 18, Monday Morning. Easter Recess.

April 14, Friday, Gage Prize Contest.

April 23, Saturday, Last day for Presentation of Theses, Advanced Degrees.

April 30, Saturday, Presentation of Dewey Prize Essays, Harris Prize Theses, and Cushing Prize Dissertations.

April 30, Saturday, Examination of Candidates for Advanced Degrees.

June 1, Wednesday, to June 9, Thursday, Regular Examinations.

June 10, Friday, Additional Examinations.

June 12, Sunday, Baccalaureate Address.

June 13 and 14,   Monday and Tuesday, Examinations for Admission to College of Liberal Arts.

June 14,   Tuesday, Kirk Prize Contest.

June 14,   Tuesday, Annual Meeting of the Phi Beta Kappa Society.

June 15,   Wednesday, Alumni Association Meeting.

June 15,   Wednesday, Annual Address before Phi Beta Kappa Society.

June 16,   Thursday, Commencement.

1897

JANUARY.

Su	Mo	Tu	W	Th	Fr	Sa
..	..	..	..	..	1	2
3	4	5	6	7	8	9
10	11	12	13	14	15	16
17	18	19	20	21	22	23
24	25	26	27	28	29	30
31	..	..	..			

JULY.

Su	Mo	Tu	W	Th	Fr	Sa
..	..	..	..	1	2	3
4	5	6	7	8	9	10
11	12	13	14	15	16	17
18	19	20	21	22	23	24
25	26	27	28	29	30	31

FEBRUARY.

Su	Mo	Tu	W	Th	Fr	Sa
..	1	2	3	4	5	6
7	8	9	10	11	12	13
14	15	16	17	18	19	20
21	22	23	24	25	26	27
28	..	..	..			

AUGUST.

Su	Mo	Tu	W	Th	Fr	Sa
1	2	3	4	5	6	7
8	9	10	11	12	13	14
15	16	17	18	19	20	21
22	23	24	25	26	27	28
29	30	31	..	..		

MARCH.

Su	Mo	Tu	W	Th	Fr	Sa
..	1	2	3	4	5	6
7	8	9	10	11	12	13
14	15	16	17	18	19	20
21	22	23	24	25	26	27
28	29	30	31	..	..	

SEPTEMBER.

Su	Mo	Tu	W	Th	Fr	Sa
..	..	..	1	2	3	4
5	6	7	8	9	10	11
12	13	14	15	16	17	18
19	20	21	22	23	24	25
26	27	28	29	30	..	..

APRIL.

Su	Mo	Tu	W	Th	Fr	Sa
..	..	..	..	1	2	3
4	5	6	7	8	9	10
11	12	13	14	15	16	17
18	19	20	21	22	23	24
25	26	27	28	29	30	..

OCTOBER.

Su	Mo	Tu	W	Th	Fr	Sa
..	..	..	..	..	1	2
3	4	5	6	7	8	9
10	11	12	13	14	15	16
17	18	19	20	21	22	23
24	25	26	27	28	29	30
31						

MAY.

Su	Mo	Tu	W	Th	Fr	Sa
..	..	..	..	..	..	1
2	3	4	5	6	7	8
9	10	11	12	13	14	15
16	17	18	19	20	21	22
23	24	25	26	27	28	29
30	31	..	..			

NOVEMBER.

Su	Mo	Tu	W	Th	Fr	Sa
..	1	2	3	4	5	6
7	8	9	10	11	12	13
14	15	16	17	18	19	20
21	22	23	24	25	26	27
28	29	30	..	..	..	

JUNE.

Su	Mo	Tu	W	Th	Fr	Sa
..	..	1	2	3	4	5
6	7	8	9	10	11	12
13	14	15	16	17	18	19
20	21	22	23	24	25	26
27	28	29	30	..	..	

DECEMBER.

Su	Mo	Tu	W	Th	Fr	Sa
..	..	..	1	2	3	4
5	6	7	8	9	10	11
12	13	14	15	16	17	18
19	20	21	22	23	24	25
26	27	28	29	30	31	..

1898

JANUARY.

Su	Mo	Tu	W	Th	Fr	Sa
..	..	..	..	..	..	1
2	3	4	5	6	7	8
9	10	11	12	13	14	15
16	17	18	19	20	21	22
23	24	25	26	27	28	29
30	31	..	..			

JULY.

Su	Mo	Tu	W	Th	Fr	Sa
..	..	..	..	..	1	2
3	4	5	6	7	8	9
10	11	12	13	14	15	16
17	18	19	20	21	22	23
24	25	26	27	28	29	30
31	..	..				

FEBRUARY.

Su	Mo	Tu	W	Th	Fr	Sa
..	..	1	2	3	4	5
6	7	8	9	10	11	12
13	14	15	16	17	18	19
20	21	22	23	24	25	26
27	28	..	..			

AUGUST.

Su	Mo	Tu	W	Th	Fr	Sa
..	1	2	3	4	5	6
7	8	9	10	11	12	13
14	15	16	17	18	19	20
21	22	23	24	25	26	27
28	29	30	31	..	..	

MARCH.

Su	Mo	Tu	W	Th	Fr	Sa
..	..	1	2	3	4	5
6	7	8	9	10	11	12
13	14	15	16	17	18	19
20	21	22	23	24	25	26
27	28	29	30	31	..	..

SEPTEMBER.

Su	Mo	Tu	W	Th	Fr	Sa
..	..	..	..	1	2	3
4	5	6	7	8	9	10
11	12	13	14	15	16	17
18	19	20	21	22	23	24
25	26	27	28	29	30	..

APRIL.

Su	Mo	Tu	W	Th	Fr	Sa
..	..	..	..	..	1	2
3	4	5	6	7	8	9
10	11	12	13	14	15	16
17	18	19	20	21	22	23
24	25	26	27	28	29	30
..	..					

OCTOBER.

Su	Mo	Tu	W	Th	Fr	Sa
..	..	..	..	..	..	1
2	3	4	5	6	7	8
9	10	11	12	13	14	15
16	17	18	19	20	21	22
23	24	25	26	27	28	29
30	31	..	..			

MAY.

Su	Mo	Tu	W	Th	Fr	Sa
1	2	3	4	5	6	7
8	9	10	11	12	13	14
15	16	17	18	19	20	21
22	23	24	25	26	27	28
29	30	31	..	..	..	

NOVEMBER.

Su	Mo	Tu	W	Th	Fr	Sa
..	..	1	2	3	4	5
6	7	8	9	10	11	12
13	14	15	16	17	18	19
20	21	22	23	24	25	26
27	28	29	30	..	..	

JUNE.

Su	Mo	Tu	W	Th	Fr	Sa
..	..	..	1	2	3	4
5	6	7	8	9	10	11
12	13	14	15	16	17	18
19	20	21	22	23	24	25
26	27	28	29	30	..	..

DECEMBER.

Su	Mo	Tu	W	Th	Fr	Sa
..	..	..	..	1	2	3
4	5	6	7	8	9	10
11	12	13	14	15	16	17
18	19	20	21	22	23	24
25	26	27	28	29	30	31

CORPORATION.

OFFICERS.

6

DAVID McWILLIAMS,	Dwight.
THE REV. RICHARD HANEY, D.D.,	Altoona.
GUSTAVUS FRANKLIN SWIFT,	Chicago.
LYMAN JUDSON GAGE,	Chicago.
THE HON. WILLIAM ANDREW DYCHE, A.M.,	Evanston.
MISS CORNELIA GRAY LUNT,	Evanston.
HENRY HOWARD GAGE,	Evanston.

TERM EXPIRES IN 1901.

NORMAN WAITE HARRIS,	Chicago.
NATHAN SMITH DAVIS, JR., A.M., M.D.,	Chicago.
ELBERT HENRY GARY,	Chicago.
GEORGE HENRY FOSTER,	Evanston.
JOHN RICHARD LINDGREN,	Evanston.
ALEXANDER HAMILTON REVELL,	Chicago.
THE HON. H. H. C. MILLER, A.M.,	Evanston.
CHARLES BUSBY,	Chicago.
MILTON HOLIDAY WILSON,	Evanston.

ELECTED BY CONFERENCES.

ROCK RIVER.

THE REV. AMOS WILLIAM PATTEN, A.M., M.D.,	Chicago.
THE REV. WILLIAM ANSON SPENCER, D.D.,	Philadelphia, Pa.

DETROIT.

THE REV. JOSEPH FLINTOFT BERRY, D.D.,	Chicago.
THE REV. ARTHUR EDWARDS, A.M., D.D.,	Chicago.

CENTRAL ILLINOIS.

THE REV. JAMES WILLIAM HANEY, A.M., D.D.,	Normal.
THE REV. FRANK WARREN MERRELL, PH.D.,	Rock Island.

MICHIGAN.

THE REV. GEORGE S. HICKEY, A.M., D.D.,	Lansing, Mich.
THE REV. ALFRED EDWIN CRAIG, A.B., B.D.,	Albion, Mich.

GENERAL EXECUTIVE COMMITTEE.

WILLIAM DEERING.	JOSIAH J. PARKHURST.
OLIVER H. HORTON, LL.D.	JOHN BALDERSTON KIRK.
FRANK PHILIP CRANDON.	JAMES HENRY RAYMOND, A.M.
HENRY WADE ROGERS, LL.D.	WILLIAM ANDREW DYCHE, A.M.
GEORGE HENRY FOSTER.	H. H. C. MILLER, A.M.

FACULTY OF LIBERAL ARTS.

Henry Wade Rogers, LL.D., President.

Daniel Bonbright, LL.D., *John Evans Professor of Latin Language and Literature.*

Oliver Marcy, LL.D., *Dean, William Deering Professor of Geology.*

Herbert Franklin Fisk, A.M., D.D., *Professor of Pedagogics.*

Robert McLean Cumnock, A.M., *Professor of Rhetoric and Elocution.*

Robert Baird, A.M., *Professor of Greek.*

Charles William Pearson, A.M., *Professor of English Literature.*

Robert Dickinson Sheppard, A.M., D.D., *Professor of English and American History.*

Abram Van Eps Young, Ph.B., *Professor of Chemistry.*

George Washington Hough, LL.D., *Professor of Astronomy and Director of Dearborn Observatory.*

James Taft Hatfield, Ph.D., *Professor of German Language and Literature.*

Charles Beach Atwell, Ph.M., *Registrar, Professor of Botany.*

Henry Crew, Ph.D., *Fayerweather Professor of Physics.*

J. Scott Clark, A.M., *Professor of English Language.*

John Henry Gray, Ph.D., *Professor of Political Science.*

Peter Christian Lutkin, *Professor of Music.*

George Albert Coe, Ph.D., *Secretary. John Evans Professor of Moral and Intellectual Philosophy.*

Charles Horswell, Ph.D., *Professor of the Hebrew Language and Literature.*

Alja Robinson Crook, Ph.D., *Professor of Mineralogy and Petrology.*

Henry Seely White, Ph.D., *Noyes Professor of Pure Mathematics.*

Thomas Franklin Holgate, Ph.D., *Professor of Applied Mathematics.*

William Caldwell, Sc.D., *Professor of Ethics and Social Philosophy.*

William Albert Locy, Ph.D., *Professor of Zoölogy.*

Charles Joseph Little, D.D., LL.D., *Professor of Church History.*

Charles Frederick Bradley, A.M., D.D., *Professor of New Testament Greek.*

George Oliver Curme, A.M., *Professor of Germanic Philology.*

James A. James, Ph.D., *Professor of the History of Continental Europe.*

Edouard Baillot, B.S., *Professor of Romance Languages.*

Emily Huntington Miller, A.M., *Principal of the Woman's Hall and Assistant Professor of English Literature.*

8

✓ HENRY COHN, A.M., *Assistant Professor of German.*
JOHN ADAMS SCOTT, PH.D., *Assistant Professor of Greek.*
MILTON SPENCER TERRY, D.D., LL.D., *Lecturer on the Bible.*
ALBERT ERICSON, A.M., *Instructor in the Swedish Language.*
NELS EDWARD SIMONSEN, A.M., D.D., *Instructor in the Norwegian and Danish Languages.*
ARTHUR HERBERT WILDE, A.B., B.D., *Instructor in History.*
MARY L. FREEMAN, A.M., *Instructor in French.*
MAURICE ALPHEUS BIGELOW, M.S., *Instructor in Zoölogy.*
OMERA FLOYD LONG, PH.D., *Instructor in Latin.*
HENRY LE DAUM, A.B., *Instructor in French.*
HORACE SNYDER, PH.D., *Assistant in Physics.*
SAMUEL DEBENHAM GLOSS, B.S., *Assistant in Chemistry.*

STANDING COMMITTEES.

Committee on College Ethics:—The PRESIDENT, Professors MARCY, BONBRIGHT, FISK, BAIRD.
Board of Examiners:—Professors WHITE, BONBRIGHT, BAIRD, CREW, BAILLOT, LOCY.
Graduate Study:—Professors BONBRIGHT, CREW, COE.
Undergraduate Study:—Professors YOUNG, HOLGATE, LOCY.
Special Students:—Professors HOLGATE, PEARSON, GRAY.
Delinquent Students:—HOLGATE, YOUNG, CALDWELL.
Academy:—Professors FISK, MARCY, CLARK.
Advanced Standing:—Professors LOCY, HATFIELD, CLARK.
Accredited Schools:—Professors JAMES, ATWELL, FISK.
Registration:—Professors ATWELL, BAIRD, CURME.
Admission Requirements:—Professors PEARSON, HOUGH, CURME.
Library:—Professors BONBRIGHT, YOUNG, LOCY.
Fellowships, Scholarships, and Charitable Funds:—Professors FISK, CALDWELL, GRAY.
Regulation of Athletic Sports:—Professors CLARK, YOUNG, WHITE.
Musical Organizations:—Professors LUTKIN, CROOK, HATFIELD.
Chapel:—Professors BAIRD, JAMES, CROOK.
Catalogue:—The PRESIDENT, The REGISTRAR, Professor CREW.

CONSULTATION HOURS.

The PRESIDENT, Daily, except Saturday, 4 to 5, Room 1, U. H.
The DEAN, - - - - Daily, 2, Room 18, U. H.
The REGISTRAR, Daily, except Saturday, 9 to 10, Room 2, U. H.
Professor BONBRIGHT, Tuesday, Wednesday, and Friday, 10 to 10:30 A. M., Room 14, U. H.
Professor FISK, - - - Daily, 11 to 12, Room 1, Academy.
Professor CUMNOCK, Monday and Tuesday, 2, Room 1, Swift Hall.

Professor BAIRD,   -   Tuesday, Wednesday and Thursday, 11, Room 12, U. H.

Professor PEARSON,   -   -   Daily, 10 to 10:30, Room 17, U. H.

Professor SHEPPARD,   Monday, Wednesday, and Friday, 4, Room 9, U. H.

Professor YOUNG,   -   -   Daily, 11 to 12, Room 21, W. S. H.

Professor HOUGH,   Tuesday and Thursday, 3, Room 4, E. S. H.

Professor CURME,   -   -   Daily, except Monday, 10 to 11.

Professor CREW,   -   -   Daily, 9 to 11, Room 10, E. S. H.

Professor CLARK,   -   -   -   Daily, 9, Room 17, U. H.

Professor GRAY,   Monday, Wednesday, and Friday, 9 to 9:45; Tuesday, 4 to 5, Room 30, Library.

Professor LUTKIN,   Monday, Tuesday, Wednesday, and Thursday, 4:30, Music Hall.

Professor COE,   Monday, Wednesday, and Friday, 3 to 3:30; Tuesday and Thursday, 2 to 3, Room 29, Library.

Professor BAILLOT, Monday and Wednesday, 3 to 4, Room 13, U. H.

Professor HORSWELL,   Tuesday and Thursday, 4, Room 10, Memorial Hall.

Professor CROOK,   -   -   Daily, 8 to 10, Room 7, W. S. H.

Professor WHITE, Monday and Wednesday, 3 to 3:30, Room 4, U. H.

Professor HOLGATE,   Tuesday and Thursday, 9 A.M., Room 4, U. H.

Professor JAMES,   Monday, Wednesday, and Friday, 10 to 10:30 Room 9, U. H.

Professor CALDWELL,   Tuesday, Wednesday, and Saturday, 10 to 11, Room 30, Library.

Professor LOCY,   Daily, except Monday and Saturday, 9 to 12, Room 25, U. H.

Professor LITTLE,   Daily, except Monday and Saturday, 10 A.M., Memorial Hall.

Professor BRADLEY,   Monday, Wednesday, and Thursday, 12:15, Memorial Hall.

Assistant Professor COHN,   Monday and Thursday, 11, Room 27, Library.

Assistant Professor SCOTT.

Rev. ALBERT ERICSON,   -   Daily, 3 to 5, Swedish Seminary.

Rev. NELS EDWARD SIMONSEN,   -   Daily, 10, Memorial Hall.

Mr. ARTHUR HERBERT WILDE,   Wednesday and Friday, 1 to 1:30, 1011 Ayars Place.

Miss MARY L. FREEMAN,   -   -   Daily, 9 to 10, Room 13, U. H.

Daily, 3 to 3:15, Room 9, U. H.

Mr. HERBERT GOVERT KEPPEL,   -   Daily, 1, Room 4, U. H.

   -    -   Tuesdays, 11, Room B, U. H.

Dr. MILTON S. TERRY,   -   Daily, 2 to 4, Room 5, Memorial Hall.

NORTHWESTERN UNIVERSITY.

The University comprises the following degree-conferring departments, each having a distinct Faculty of Instruction:

THE COLLEGE OF LIBERAL ARTS,
THE MEDICAL SCHOOL,
THE LAW SCHOOL,
THE SCHOOL OF PHARMACY,
THE DENTAL SCHOOL,
THE WOMAN'S MEDICAL SCHOOL,
THE SCHOOL OF MUSIC,
THE SCHOOLS OF THEOLOGY.

The College of Liberal Arts represents the collegiate side of University work, as distinguished from the work of the professional schools. Its courses of instruction are arranged to meet the wants of students who, having completed the work of an academy or high school, are prepared to take up a systematic or advanced course of study. It is designed to afford such a disciplinary and general education as constitutes a solid foundation for future professional work. It is also intended to provide the liberal culture which is commended as an end in itself to men and women, whatever course in life they may expect to pursue. It offers both undergraduate and graduate courses of instruction.

Special students who wish to pursue selected studies without reference to the attainment of a degree are also admitted on conditions hereafter to be stated.

UNIVERSITY STATUTES.

The following statutes have been adopted by the Trustees:

PRESIDENT. The President of the University shall be the head of the educational departments of the University, and of each of them. He shall see that all the rules and regulations prescribed by the

Board of Trustees or the Executive Committee for the government of the University are faithfully observed. He shall exercise such general executive powers as are necessary to the good government of the University and the protection of its interests, and which are not otherwise provided for.

It shall be his duty to nominate to the Board officers of instruction, except as otherwise provided, and to see that all officers of instruction are doing a proper amount and a satisfactory quality of work.

He shall prepare an annual report on the condition and needs of the University, shall cause the same to be printed, and shall send a copy to each member of the Board prior to its annual meeting.

He shall be, whenever present, the presiding officer of the Faculty of any College or School of the University. He shall have the right of a deciding vote in case of a tie. He shall appoint all committees provided for by the Faculty, unless otherwise ordered, and shall call extra meetings of any Faculty, whenever, in his judgment, such meetings may be called for by the welfare of the University.

OFFICERS. The officers of instruction in the University shall have designation and preference as follows :

1. Professors.
2. Acting Professors.
3. Associate Professors.
4. Assistant Professors.
5. Instructors.
6. Tutors.
7. Lecturers.
8. Such other subordinate officers as may be from time to time appointed.

FACULTIES. The Faculty of any College or School shall be constituted of officers of instruction who are above the rank of Tutor.

Each department of study shall be under the supervision of a Professor or Acting Professor, who shall be the head of the department, and who, subject to the direction of the Faculty, shall have final decision in all matters relating to the work of the department. In case there shall be two or more officers having the rank of Professor in any department, the one first appointed shall have precedence.

Each Faculty shall have power to determine the requirements for the admission of students to such departments of the University as are under its jurisdiction; to prescribe and define the various courses of study for undergraduate and graduate students; to determine, subject to revision by the Board of Trustees, the requirements for such degrees as are offered to students under its jurisdiction; to enact and enforce such rules for the guidance and government of its own students as it may deem best adapted to the interests of the University.

There shall be elected by the Board of Trustees or the Executive Committee a Dean of each School or College, whose duty it shall be to preside at all meetings of the Faculty of such School or College in the absence of the President of the University. He shall annually submit to the President of the University, not later than June 1, a report of the work of the School or College to which he belongs, with such recommendations as he may deem advisable, and the reports so made may be made a part of the President's annual report to the Board of Trustees.

Each Faculty may present at any meeting of the Board or of the Executive Committee a report of any matters concerning the interests of its School or College, which report shall be transmitted through the President of the University.

No officer in the University shall absent himself from the discharge of his proper duties in the University longer than three college days at any one time without securing the previous consent of the President of the University or of the Dean of the School to which said officer of instruction belongs; but this rule shall not be applied in case of absence occasioned by sickness, or death of relatives.

A Committee for the Regulation of Athletic Sports shall hereafter be annually appointed and chosen as follows: Three members of the University Faculties and three alumni of the University, these six to be appointed by the Executive Committee, and also three undergraduates, to be chosen during the first week of the College of Liberal Arts year by the Athletic Association. This committee shall have entire supervision and control of all athletic exercises within and without the precincts of the University, subject to the authority of the Faculty of Liberal Arts.

DUTIES AND DISCIPLINE OF STUDENTS. All students are required to obey the rules of the University, to comply with the rules and regulations made by the Faculty of the School or College to which they belong, and to conduct themselves at all times with decorum and propriety.

Any student who is sent for by the President or any officer of instruction of the Faculty under which he is enrolled shall comply with the call without delay, and students must at all times obey the directions of the President or any officer of instruction in the School or College to which they belong, pertaining to good order in the institution.

A student may be suspended, dismissed, or expelled by a vote of two-thirds of the Professors of the Faculty of the School or College in which he is a member, provided always that, prior to such contemplated suspension, dismission, or expulsion, he be granted the right to a full and impartial hearing before the Faculty, and in all cases of discipline contemplating suspension, dismission, or expulsion the vote shall be by ballot. In the Academy this power of discipline shall belong to the Faculty of Liberal Arts.

Concerted absence from any appointed duty by a class or by any number of students together will be regarded as a violation of good order, and will be followed by suspension, dismission, or expulsion, at the discretion of the Faculty.

When any Faculty shall become satisfied that a student is not fulfilling the purpose of his residence at the University, or is for any cause an unfit member thereof, the President shall notify his parents or guardians, that they may have an opportunity to withdraw him, and if he is not withdrawn within a reasonable time he shall be dismissed. *

Students or societies in the University are forbidden to invite any lecturer to address them in public until the name of the proposed lecturer shall have been presented to the President of the University or to the Dean of the School to which such students or societies belong, and his permission to extend the invitation has been obtained.

Publication by any student or students of any paper or production bearing the name of the University, or purporting to issue from it, is forbidden, unless the publication is previously approved by the President.

Women students in the College of Liberal Arts or in the Academy, who are not residents of Evanston, are required to live in Woman's Hall or in the College Cottage, unless special permission shall be granted them to live elsewhere. Application for such permission shall be determined by a committee which shall consist of the President of the University, the Principal of the Academy, the Principal of Woman's Hall, and the Business Agent of the University.

Excursions upon Lake Michigan in steamers or other vessels by bodies of students in departments of the University situated in Evanston, shall not be planned or carried out without the consent of the President or the Executive Committee, which consent shall not be given until all possible precautions for the safety of the excursion party have been taken under the direction of a competent University representative.

The Oxford cap and gown shall be worn as an official dress at Commencement.

GRADUATION. All degrees in this institution, except honorary degrees, shall be conferred by the Board of Trustees on the recommendation of the proper Faculty; honorary degrees may be conferred upon the recommendation of the University Council.

Prior to the Commencement of any School or College, the Faculty thereof shall report to the Board of Trustees, if that Board is in session, the names in full and the places of residence of all students whom they shall recommend for degrees, whereupon the Board shall, in its discretion, pass a resolution to confer the same. In case the Board shall not be in session, the Faculty shall report the names as aforesaid to the Executive Committee of the Board of Trustees, who shall recommend that the President confer the degrees and report the same to the Board of Trustees for its approval.

For the recommendation of students to degrees by the different Faculties, all votes shall be by ballot. All candidates for degrees, except honorary degrees, shall be personally present at Commencement exercises, unless the Board or Executive Committee, on the recommendation of the appropriate Faculty, shall deem it proper to confer the degree in the absence of the candidate; and the candidate shall perform such public duties on Commencement day as the Faculty may designate.

The name of no person shall be presented for a degree till all his dues to the University are paid. No fee shall be charged for an honorary degree.

All degrees shall be conferred by the President on the authority of the Board of Trustees.

No duplicate diplomas shall be granted to graduates of the University without such proof of the loss of the original by affidavit or otherwise as shall be satisfactory to the Executive Committee.

THE UNIVERSITY COUNCIL. The President of the University, together with the Dean of each Faculty, and another member thereof elected annually by the Faculty, shall constitute the University Council.

The University Council shall meet on the day preceding the annual meeting of the Board of Trustees, and at such other times as the President of the University may designate.

The University Council may consider such matters as pertain to the interests of the University as a whole, and may make recommendations concerning the same to the Board of Trustees.

The University Council may recommend to the Board of Trustees the person or persons upon whom they think it desirable that honorary degrees should be conferred.

CANDIDATES FOR ADMISSION.

Candidates for admission to the College of Liberal Arts must be at least sixteen years of age, and must present to the Registrar satisfactory evidence of good moral character, together with credentials from their last instructors, or from the institution in which they were prepared. They must pay the matriculation fee before taking the entrance examinations.

ADMISSION OF CANDIDATES FOR A DEGREE.

Candidates for admission who expect to apply for a bachelor's degree must show satisfactory evidence of preparation in the following subjects, either by examination or by certificate from an accredited school:—namely,

(1) All the subjects included in Group A.

(2) Six items from Groups B and C, of which at least four must be from Group B.

NOTE.—The alternative of presenting a certificate or passing an examination is offered in all studies except English. This exception is made because of the paramount importance of a thorough mastery of the chief medium of instruction and also because of the comparative neglect of the mother tongue in some schools, it being often erroneously assumed that a sufficient knowledge of English will be easily and incidentally acquired. Accordingly, after October 1, 1897, no certificate will be accepted from any candidate in place of an examination in the English language.

GROUP A.

1. *English Language*—Candidates will be expected to show, by an original composition on some simple subject, prescribed at the time, a fair knowledge of grammatical construction and of good literary form. Stress is laid upon spelling, etymology, definition, capitalization, punctuation, paragraphing, italicizing, and the use of quotation marks. The candidate's knowledge of form will also be tested by assigning to him a selection from some well-edited paper or magazine, and asking him to give a clear reason for the use of every capital, punctuation mark, etc., found in that section. *Time requirement, two hours a week throughout one year.*

2. *English Literature*—The candidate is expected to read intelligently all the books prescribed below. He should read them as he reads other books; he is not expected to know them minutely, but to

have them freshly in mind, and be able to write an essay showing familiarity with the plot, incidents, and characters of each work.

For 1897 the works are: Shakespeare's Merchant of Venice and As You Like It; Defoe's History of the Plague in London; Irving's Tales of a Traveller; Hawthorne's Twice-Told Tales; Longfellow's Evangeline; George Eliot's Silas Marner; Burke's Conciliation with America; Scott's Marmion; Macaulay's Life of Samuel Johnson.

In and after 1898, the examination in English Literature will be conducted as follows:

I. Reading.—A certain number of books will be set for reading. The candidate will be required to present evidence of a general knowledge of the subject-matter, and to answer simple questions on the lives of the authors. The form of examination will usually be the writing of a paragraph or two on each of several topics, to be chosen by the candidate from a considerable number—perhaps ten or fifteen—set before him in the examination paper. The treatment of these topics is designed to test the candidate's power of clear and accurate expression, and will call for only a general knowledge of the substance of the books. In place of a part or the whole of this test, the candidate may present an exercise book, properly certified by his instructor, containing compositions or other written work done in connection with the reading of the books.

The books set for this part of the examination will be:

1898: Milton's Paradise Lost, Books I and II; Pope's Iliad, Books I, VI, XXII and XXIV; The Sir Roger de Coverley Papers in the Spectator; Goldsmith's Vicar of Wakefield; Coleridge's Ancient Mariner; Southey's Life of Nelson; Carlyle's Essay on Burns; Lowell's Vision of Sir Launfal; Hawthorne's The House of Seven Gables.

1899: Dryden's Palamon and Arcite; Pope's Iliad, Books I, VI, XXII and XXIV; The Sir Roger de Coverley Papers in the Spectator; Goldsmith's Vicar of Wakefield; Coleridge's Ancient Mariner; De Quincey's Flight of a Tartar Tribe; Cooper's Last of the Mohicans; Lowell's Vision of Sir Launfal; Hawthorne's The House of Seven Gables.

1900: Dryden's Palamon and Arcite; Pope's Iliad, Books I, VI, XXII and XXIV; The Sir Roger de Coverley Papers; Vicar of Wakefield; Ivanhoe; De Quincey's Flight of a Tartar Tribe; Cooper's Last of the Mohicans; Tennyson's Princess; Lowell's Vision of Sir Launfal.

II: Study and Practice.—This part of the examination presupposes the thorough study of each of the works named below. The examination will be upon the subject-matter, form and structure.

The books set for this part of the examination will be:

1898: Shakespeare's Macbeth; Burke's Speech on Conciliation with America; De Quincey's Flight of a Tartar Tribe; Tennyson's Princess.

1899: Macbeth; Paradise Lost, Books I and II; Burke's Speech on Conciliation with America; Carlyle's Essay on Burns.

1900: Macbeth; Paradise Lost, Books I and II; Burke's Speech on Conciliation with America; Macaulay's Essays on Milton and Addison.

3. *Mathematics*—Wentworth's School Algebra or Wells' Academic Algebra, through Radicals and Quadratics or an equivalent; Plane and Solid Geometry. *Time requirement, five hours a week for two years.*

4. *Human Anatomy and Physiology* — Martin's Human Body (Briefer Course). *Time requirement, five hours a week, one-third of a year.*

5. *Geography*—Tarr's Physical Geography. The candidate must be able to draw an outline map of any country or state, and locate therein the principal towns, rivers, and mountains. *Time requirement, five hours a week, one-third of a year.*

6. *History*—(a) Smith's Smaller History of Greece, or an equivalent; Allen's History of Rome, or an equivalent; or (b) General History, Myers, or an equivalent. *Time requirement in each, five hours a week, two-thirds of a year.*

7. *History of the United States* -- Johnston's or an equivalent. *Time requirement, five hours a week, one-third of a year.*

Group B.

11. *Greek*—(a) Grammar, White's Beginner's Greek Book, or an equivalent; Xenophon's Anabasis, first book; Jones' Greek Composition, lessons 1–10, or the first book in Woodruff's Greek Prose Composition. *Time requirement, five hours a week throughout one year.*

12. *Greek* (b) Xenophon's Anabasis, books second, third and fourth, or an equivalent of Xenophon's Hellenica; Homer, the Odyssey or Iliad, 1,800 lines; Greek Composition, Jones's Lessons, 11–40, or an equivalent in Woodruff's Greek Prose Composition. *Time requirement, five hours a week throughout one year.*

13. *Latin* (a) Grammar; Cæsar's Gallic War, ten pages, or twenty pages of Viri Romæ, with re-translation of English into Latin. *Time requirement, five hours a week throughout one year.*

14. *Latin* (b) Cæsar's Gallic War, four books completed; or Viri Romæ, completed; Latin Composition. *Time requirement, five hours a week throughout one year.*

15. *Latin (c)* Cicero, six orations, including the Manilian Law; Latin Composition. *Time requirement, five hours a week throughout one year.*

16. *Latin (d)* Vergil, eight books of the Æneid, or six books of the Æneid and the Bucolics. *Time requirement, five hours a week throughout one year.*

17. *French (a)* Grammar (Whitney or Edgren); Grandgent's Composition, one book; selections of modern prose and poetry, not less in quantity than four hundred and fifty pages. From students offering no composition work, more reading will be required. A thorough knowledge of irregular verbs, rules of past participle, etc., is expected; also the ability to translate simple spoken French phrases and to translate at sight ordinary prose. As far as possible the reading should be complete works, not short selections, and one modern comedy should be read. *Two years of high school work will usually be required for this course.*

18. *French (b)* includes: Proficiency in advanced grammar, use of moods and tenses, government of infinitives and ordinary idioms; Composition (Grandgent, Parts III, IV, and V, or an equivalent); reading of not less than 1,200 duodecimo pages of at least five standard authors; ability to understand questions and phrases in French, and to take grammatical dictations. *Time requirement, five hours a week throughout one year.*

19. *German (a)* Elementary Grammar, especially declension of articles and ordinary nouns and pronouns, use of the strong and weak adjective, the old and new verbs, separable and inseparable prefixes, the use of common prepositions, the inverted and transposed sentence-order. For this work, Otis's Elementary German, Part I, contains sufficient material. Practice in writing German sentences should accompany the course throughout.

The reading of at least two hundred pages of material of a narrative or epic nature. Good material is offered by Brandt's or Joynes's Reader, Grimm's or Andersen's Märchen, Uhland's Ballads, or Niebuhr's Heroen-Geschichten.

20. *German (b)* Advanced Grammar, especially the syntax of cases, the special uses of modal and other auxiliaries, uses of the subjunctive, complex sentence-construction, word-formation. The systematic writing of connected German narrative prose should have given the ability to write simple German. In addition to the requirement under (a) should be read at least five hundred pages of material which appeals to the historic and dramatic sense, as well as to a feeling for rhythm and poetical form. Recommended are: The less difficult standard dramas, as Minna von Barnhelm, Tell, or Marie Stuart; Riehl's Novellen; Freytag's Soll und Haben (abridged);

Goethe's Hermann und Dorothea, and the easier lyrics of such poets as Goethe, Schiller, Geibel, Heine, Rückert and Platen.

Courses (a) and (b) together will usually be done best by high schools in three years.

GROUP C.

The time requirement for each subject in this group is five hours a week for one year.

21. *Mathematics*—Includes: Algebra, as much as is contained in Wentworth's College Algebra, chapters 16–27, inclusive, and chapter 29; Plane Trigonometry, including the solution of Triangles, Wentworth's, or an equivalent.

22. *Physics*—Gage's Elementary Physics or Carhart and Chute's Elements of Physics entire, or an equivalent.

23. *Dynamics*—Lodge's Elementary Mechanics, or an equivalent. Instruction in this subject must have been accompanied by experimental work.

NOTE.—Students are earnestly recommended not to attempt to cover the whole field of Physics, but to offer more thorough preparation in Dynamics, including Pneumatics, Hydrostatics, and Water Waves.

Students thus prepared will, on entrance at College, be able to go ahead with the subject of Physics, as they are with Latin, Greek, or Mathematics. Those, however, who have covered the whole ground of Physics find it, in general, necessary to retrace their steps if the study is taken up again at college.

24. *General Chemistry and the introduction to Qualitative Analysis*— The first part of this requirement would be met by the first ten chapters of Cooke's New Chemistry, with the Laboratory Practice by the same author, or by Remsen's Briefer Course, or by Sheppard's Elements. The second part would require the analysis of five mixtures, involving third, fourth, and fifth group metals (Prescott and Johnson). Laboratory work with the candidate's original note-book will be essential in meeting this requirement, which is made equivalent to Chemistry A in college, and thus qualifies the student to take Chemistry B.

25. *Biology*—One year's study of typical animals and plants by laboratory methods covering the facts of morphology and physiology. This requirement may be met by a course such as that laid down in Boyer's Elementary Biology, or in Colton's Practical Zoölogy, and Bergen's Elements of Botany. Laboratory notes and drawings must be presented.

Instead of one year's preparation in Physics, Chemistry or Biology, the equivalent of four terms' work, each of five hours a week from the subjects in Group D will be accepted when necessary, but students are strongly advised, whenever it is possible, to make choice of one subject and pursue it through the year.

GROUP D.

31. *Botany*—A practical knowledge of the general facts of vegetable morphology, physiology and classification, such a course as is outlined in Bergen's Elements of Botany or Boyer's Elementary Biology, Part II. Laboratory drawings and notes must be presented.

32. *Zoölogy* — A study of various animal types founded upon laboratory work such as that prescribed in Part I, Boyer's Elementary Biology. Laboratory notes and drawings must be presented.

33. *Physics*—Gage's Elements, first two chapters or an equivalent.

34. *Astronomy*—Young's Elements.

35. *Geology*—Le Conte's Elements.

36. *Chemistry*—Remsen's Elementary Course, or an equivalent. It is urgently recommended that laboratory work by the student accompany this study. The laboratory note-books must be presented by the candidate with his credentials.

37. *Drawing*—Elements of Free-Hand and Geometrical Drawing; such a knowledge of the subject as may be gained by practice under instruction two hours a week through one year.

38. *History of England*—Montgomery's, or an equivalent.

39. *Civil Government*—Fiske's, or an equivalent.

EXAMINATION FOR ADMISSION.

The regular days of examination for admission to the College of Liberal Arts are the Monday and Tuesday next before Commencement, and the Monday and Tuesday next before the opening of the college year. The first regular examination for the year 1897 was held on June 14 and 15; the second will be held on September 20 and 21. Candidates may be examined and admitted at other times, if prepared to enter classes at an advanced point in the regular courses; they are advised, however, to enter at the beginning of a year.

Upon the dates above named, examinations will be held in the following order in Room 10, University Hall.

PLAN FOR ENTRANCE EXAMINATIONS, 1897.

MONDAY, JUNE 14 AND SEPT. 20.

8 A.M., Subjects 12, 18, 19, 21, 22, 27, 28.

10 A.M., Subjects 14, 15, 23, 24, 31, 33.

2 P.M., Subject 4.

3 P.M., Subject 5.

4 P.M., Subjects 13, 35, 16.

TUESDAY, JUNE 15 AND SEPT. 21.

8 A.M., Subject 3.

10 A.M., Subjects 6, 29.

11 A.M., Subjects 11, 25, 26, 30, 34, 35.

2 P.M., Subject 1.

3 P.M., Subject 2.

4 P.M., Subject 7.

Examinations for admission are held in Evanston at the times above named. By special arrangement with the President, examinations may also be held at St. Paul, Minnesota; Denver, Colorado; Omaha, Nebraska; St. Louis, Missouri; Cincinnati, Ohio; Detroit, Michigan; Portland, Oregon; and San Francisco, California. But in all such cases application must be made to the President prior to June 1st.

CERTIFICATES.

Candidates for admission are required to bring from their teachers certificates giving in detail the amount and grade of their preparatory work, but such certificates will not be accepted for studies pursued in college. Blanks of the proper form should be obtained from the University by application to the Registrar.

ADMISSION FROM ACCREDITED SCHOOLS.

Students who come from an accredited academy or high school may be admitted on certificate without examination, provided they present themselves for admission not later than a year and three months after their graduation. Any student applying for admission without examination must present to the Board of Examiners a certificate from the principal or school superintendent, recommending him for admission to the University. This certificate must show the studies pursued in the school, the time spent in each, the text-book or manual used, the extent of work covered, the grade of the student's work, and the date (approximate) of the final examination. It will be most convenient to use for this certificate a blank form furnished by the University, as mentioned above.

It should be clearly understood that students are admitted

on certificate from accredited schools upon this condition, that *if the work of the student in his first semester shall prove unsatisfactory he may be required to enter a fitting school and review his preparation in the study in which the failure has occurred.*

ACCREDITED SCHOOLS.

School-boards desiring to have their schools placed on the accredited list should make application to the President of the University, who will provide, if practicable, for a proper inspection by committee. The following information will be expected in the letter of application:

a. The names of all the teachers, with a statement both of their preparation for teaching and of their experience in that work.

b. The latest printed catalogue or annual report of the school, containing an outline of the course of study and text-books used.

c. A careful statement of the methods pursued in teaching Mathematics, Language, and the Sciences.

d. The amount and kind of scientific apparatus and the extent of library facilities accessible to students.

The committee of inspection will ordinarily consist of members of the Faculty, but, in cases where the school is so distant from the seat of the University as to make this impracticable, other persons may be appointed to perform the work of inspection under the direction of the Faculty. The traveling expenses of the committee of inspection are borne by the school or schools visited.

The schools which are approved by the Faculty after inspection will be placed on the accredited list, and the relation thus established will continue for three years, unless the Faculty within this period becomes satisfied that such changes have occurred as make further inspection desirable.

The following schools are now on the accredited list:

SCHOOL.	PRINCIPAL.
Aurora, High School, East,	W. J. Pringle.
Aurora, High School, West,	Miss Kate Reynolds.
Austin, High School,	B. F. Buck.
Beloit, Wis., Academy,	Rev. A. W. Burr, M.A.
Beloit, Wis., High School,	A. R. Whitson, B.S.

SCHOOL.	PRINCIPAL.
Belvidere, North Side High School,	H. A. Warren.
Belvidere, South Side High School,	A. J. Snyder.
Chicago, Allen Academy,	Ira W. Allen, A.M., LL.D.
Chicago, Englewood High School,	J. E. Armstrong.
Chicago, Harvard School,	J. J. Schobinger.
Chicago, Hyde Park High School,	Chas. W. French.
Chicago, Jefferson High School,	Chas. A. Cook.
Chicago, Lake High School,	E. F. Stearns.
Chicago, Lake View High School,	Jas. H. Norton.
Chicago, North Div. High School,	O. S. Westcott.
Chicago, Northwest Div. High School,	Franklin P. Fisk.
Chicago, West. Div. High School,	Geo. M. Clayberg.
Chicago, South Div. High School,	Jeremiah Slocum.
Chicago, South Side Academy,	Edward O. Sisson, A.B.
Clinton, Ia., High School,	Miss Julia A. Sweet.
Crown Point, Ind., High School,	G. Voorhees.
Des Moines, Ia., High School,	Frank E. Plummer.
Decatur, High School,	Louis B. Lee.
Evanston, Township High School,	H. L. Boltwood, A.M.
Evanston, University Academy,	Rev. H. F. Fisk, A.M., D.D.
Elgin, Academy,	A. G. Welch, A.M.
Elgin, High School,	Walter W. Lewis.
Freeport, High School,	J. E. McGilvery.
Fond du Lac, Wis., High School,	Edward McLaughlin.
Geneseo, High School,	Miss Ada Schnabele.
Harvey, High School,	J. E. Cable.
Indianapolis, Ind., High Schools,	Geo. W. Hufford, Chas. E. Emmerich.
Joliet, High School,	J. Stanley Brown.
Kansas City, Mo., High School,	Jno. T. Buchanan.
Keokuk, Ia., High School,	G. E. Manhall.
Kewanee, High School,	H. S. Latham.
Kidder, Mo., Kidder Institute,	G. W. Shaw, M.A.
Lake Geneva, Wis., High School,	A. F. Bartlett.
Marengo High School,	C. W. Hart.
Maryville, Mo., Maryville Seminary,	Geo. E. Moore, A.M.
Milwaukee, Wis., Academy,	Julius H. Pratt, Ph.D.
Milwaukee, Wis., High Schools,	Supt. H. O. R. Siefert.
Minneapolis, Minn., High School,	J. N. Greer.
Muscatine, Ia., High School,	E. F. Schall.
Moline High School,	F. A. Manny.
Oak Park, High School,	D. O. Barto.
Onarga, Grand Prairie Seminary,	S. Van Pelt.

Orchard Lake, Mich., Military Academy,	Wm. H. Butts, A.M.
Ottawa, High School,	J. O. Leslie, A.M.
Peoria, High School,	A. W. Beasley.
Princeton, High School,	Richard A. Metcalf, A.M.
Racine, Wis., High School,	A. J. Volland.
Rock Island, High School,	W. N. Halsey.
Rockford College,	Miss Sarah F. Anderson.
Rockford, High School,	B. D. Parker.
Sioux City, Ia., High School,	C. A. Miller.
Springfield, High School,	W. W. Helmle.
Sterling, High School,	Miss Anna Parmelee.
Streator, Township High School,	J. W. Coultas.
Warren, Warren Academy,	Ida M. Gardner, A.M.
Warren, Penn., High School,	W. G. Haupt, A.M.
Waukegan, High School,	F. H. Hall.
Wheaton, High School,	H. O. Staufft.
Whitewater, Wis., High School.	C. H. Sylvester.
Wichita, Kansas, High School,	Frank H. Dyer.

Schools in California, Iowa, Indiana, Kansas, Michigan, Minnesota, and Wisconsin that are on the accredited list of the State Universities of their respective states will be recognized as if accredited by this University.

ADMISSION OF SPECIAL STUDENTS.

Persons desiring to pursue studies in the College of Liberal Arts are, as a rule, required to pass the entrance examinations prescribed for candidates for some one of the degrees, as described on previous pages. But under exceptional circumstances persons of serious purpose who are not candidates for a degree may be admitted as special students and allowed to pursue selected studies. Any one desiring to be so admitted will be furnished by the Registrar with blank forms of application, which must be filled out and presented to the Committee on Special Students, who will decide upon the advisability of granting the application. Such applications must be accompanied by the regular entrance fee and by evidence of sufficient qualification to carry on the proposed work to advantage. The college work of all students so admitted is under the supervision of the Committee on Special Students.

ADMISSION TO ADVANCED STANDING.

Candidates for advanced standing are not admitted later than September of the collegiate year in which they expect to graduate. All students from other colleges must present evidence of honorable dismission, and must give satisfactory proof of preparation for the courses which they desire to enter. The amount of College credit to be obtained by certificate from another institution is determined by a standing committee of the faculty, but no advanced credit will be given without examination except for work done in an approved college.

No student will be recommended for a Bachelor's degree until satisfactory credit has been obtained for at least one full year of work in residence at this institution.

ADMISSION OF WOMEN.

Women have been admitted to the College of Liberal Arts since 1869 on the same conditions as men. They attend the same classes and receive the same degrees as the men. Women students, however, are required to live either in Woman's Hall or in the College Cottage, unless they obtain permission to live elsewhere. If such permission is desired they must make formal application therefor. Blanks for this purpose can be obtained from the Principal of Woman's Hall, or from the Registrar.

For the purpose of giving Woman's Hall the safeguards of a well-ordered home, and of bringing those residing in it as far as possible under family influence, the authorities of the University have committed the immediate oversight of it to a Principal, who lives at the Hall, associates with the residents, and acts toward them at all times as a friend and adviser. It is intended that the Principal shall always be a woman of high character and attainments, who can give suggestions to the young women as to their general culture, advise them in social matters, and give them, in special cases, such counsel as circumstances may require.

For young women who do not wish to incur the expense incident to living at Woman's Hall, provision is made at what is known as the College Cottage. This is in charge of an association of ladies, incorporated as The Woman's Educational Aid Association, whose duty is to canvass the claims of all applicants for admission, and to have a friendly supervision over them while members of the Cottage family. The ordinary work of the Cottage is done by the young women under the direction of a competent Matron. In this way the expenses of living are materially reduced.

All women students, wherever they reside, are expected to conform as nearly as possible to the general regulations prescribed for the conduct of those living at Woman's Hall.

NOTE.—For further information respecting Woman's Hall, letters of inquiry should be addressed to Mrs. Emily Huntington Miller, Principal, Evanston, Ill.; and for information respecting the College Cottage, letters should be addressed to Mrs. J. A. Pearsons, President of the Woman's Educational Aid Association, Evanston, Ill.

PROGRAMS OF STUDY.

NOTE.—The annual courses designated by capital letters are hereinafter described. The time assignment is in hours a week for a year (three terms).

As a condition of graduation, the student is required to complete 120 semester-hours. Four years will usually be necessary for the satisfactory accomplishment of the work. From the various courses of study offered, the student is permitted to make his elections, subject to certain prescribed programs.

Prescribed courses must take precedence of elective courses, and in the order designated in the programs. Modifications of these programs, desirable because of substitutions allowed in entrance requirements, may be made at the time of registration, but the full amount of required work must be completed before graduation. Having begun an elective course the student will be expected to continue it through the year.

The programs of prescribed annual courses leading to the several degrees are as follows:

BACHELOR OF ARTS.

First Year.—Greek A, five hours; Latin A, five hours; Mathematics A, four hours, or AB, five hours; Elocution A, two hours.

Second Year.—Greek B, three hours; Latin B, three hours; Mathematics B, or C, three hours; French AA, five hours, or German AB, four hours (required only of those who entered without credit in French or in German); English Language A, two hours.

Third Year.—English Literature F, one hour.

Fourth Year.—Philosophy B, one hour.

NOTE.—On the completion of the courses Greek A, Latin A, and Mathematics A, or AB, the student may, if he desires, discontinue one of these three subjects and substitute for it elective work of not less than three hours. For those who enter without Greek, courses (*a*) and (*b*) in Greek (p. 18) become prescribed work, to be completed before taking Greek A.

BACHELOR OF PHILOSOPHY.

First Year.—French A, five hours (for those who entered with French (*a*), p. 19), or French B, three hours (for those who entered with both French (*a*) and (*b*) p 19), or German A, five hours (for those who entered with German (*a*), p. 19), or German B, three hours (for those who entered with both German (*a*) and (*b*) p. 19); Latin A or Greek A, five hours; Mathematics A, four hours, or AB, five hours; Elocution A, two hours.

Second Year.—French B, or German B, three hours (according to amount of credit already obtained in French or German); Latin B, or Greek B, three hours; Mathematics, B or C, three hours; French AB, five hours (for those who entered without French), or German AB, four hours (for those who entered without German); English Language A, two hours.

Third Year.—English Literature F, one hour.

Fourth Year.—Philosophy B, one hour.

NOTE.—On the completion of Greek A or Latin A, and Mathematics A or AB, and French A or German A, the student may, if he desire, discontinue one of these three subjects, and substitute for it elective work of not less than three hours. For those who enter without Greek and desire to elect Greek in the options above indicated, the courses (*a*) and (*b*) in Greek (p. 18) become prescribed work, to be completed before taking Greek A.

BACHELOR OF SCIENCE.

First Year.—French AA, or A, or German AB, four hours, or A, five hours (according to amount of credit already obtained in French and German); Mathematics AB, five hours; Chemistry A, or Zoölogy A, four hours; Elocution A, two hours.

Second Year.—French AA, or A, or German AB, four hours, or A, five hours (according to amount of credit already obtained in French and German); Zoölogy B, two hours; English Language A, two hours.

Third Year.—English Literature F, one hour; Physics A, four hours, or Chemistry A, four hours, or Zoölogy A, four hours (two of these being prescribed in this program).

Fourth Year.—Philosophy B, one hour.

NOTE.—The completion of courses AA and A, in French, or their equivalent, and of courses AB and A, in German, or their equivalent, either before or after admission to college, is a requirement for this degree.

BACHELOR OF LETTERS.

First Year.—French A A, five hours, for those who entered without French, or French A, five hours, for those who entered with French (*a*), or French B, three hours, for those who entered with French (*a*) and (*b*); German AB, four hours, for those who entered without German (*a*), or German A, five hours, for those who entered with German (*a*), or German B, three hours, for those who entered with German (*a*) and (*b*); Mathematics A, four hours, or AB, five hours; Elocution A, two hours.

Second Year.—French A, five hours, or French B, three hours (according to the amount of credit in French already obtained); German A, five hours, or German B, three hours (according to the amount of credit in German already obtained); English Literature A, five hours; English Language A, two hours.

Third Year.—English Language B, two hours.

Fourth Year.—Philosophy B, one hour.

NOTE.—The completion of courses AA, and A, and B, or their equivalent, in French; and of courses AB, and A, and B, or their equivalent, in German, either in preparation or in college, is a requirement for this degree.

COURSES OF INSTRUCTION.

EXPLANATORY NOTE.—Year-courses, *i.e.*, courses continuous through the two terms of the year, are designated by capital letters. Arabic numerals are inserted for convenience of reference, one unit being allowed for each of the two terms in the college year.

ASTRONOMY AND METEOROLOGY.

A—1. Young's General Astronomy.
  2. Meteorology.
      Tuesday, Thursday, 2. Two hours. Professor HOUGH.

THE BIBLE.

A—1. The Old Testament Canon; ancient and modern versions of the Bible.
  Critical study and analysis of the most important Books of the Old Testament. Lectures.

2. Introduction to and critical study of the New Testament. Lectures.
Wednesday, 4. One hour.   Professor TERRY.

B—3. Expository lectures upon selected Prophetical Books of the Old Testament.
Expository lectures upon selected Psalms and Epistles.

4. Expository lectures upon the Revelation of John.
Monday, 4. One hour.   Professor TERRY.
These courses are ordinarily given in alternate years, but will be omitted in 1897–98.

BOTANY.

A—1. An introductory course, which consists of individual investigation of the morphology and life-cycles of typical plants selected from seven of the more important natural groups. Laboratory work and lectures.

2. Structure and Morphology of Flowering Plants. Systematic Botany. Recitations and field-work.
Monday, Friday, 2-4; Wednesday, 3. Three hours.
Professor ATWELL.

B—3. Cryptogams. Morphology of the Algæ and Fungi. Laboratory-work and lectures.

4. Morphology of Mosses and Ferns. Laboratory-work and lectures.
Daily at 11. Three hours.   Professor ATWELL.

C—5. Bacteria, and Special Problems. The course involves original work. Extra hours at irregular intervals will be necessary.

6. Physiology of Plants. Experimental laboratory-work. This course must be preceded by at least one other course in Botany. Chemistry A is also advised as a preliminary course.
Tuesday, Thursday, 2-4. Two hours. Professor ATWELL.

D—7. Botanical Club. Instructors and advanced students will report and discuss important articles in botanical literature.
Wednesday, 4. One hour.   Professor ATWELL.

CHEMISTRY.

A—1 and 2. General Chemistry, lectures and laboratory work and Introduction to Qualitative Analysis.
Section I., Tuesday, Wednesday, Thursday, 1:30-4.
Section II., Monday, Friday, 2:30-5, Tuesday and Thursday, 1:30-2:30. Four hours.   Professor YOUNG.

B—3 and 4.   Qualitative Analysis, continued and Organic Chem·
istry, lectures, text and laboratory-work.
Course B open to those who have completed A.
Monday, Friday, 1:30-4, Wednesday 2-5. Four hours.
                                     Professor YOUNG.

C—5 and 6.   Quantitative Analysis, Gravimetric and Volumetric.
Course C open to those who have completed A.
*Tuesday, Thursday, 1:30-4:30, Wednesday, 10-12. Four
hours.*   Professor YOUNG.

D—7 and 8.   Problems in the application of Qualitative and Quan-
titative Analysis.
Course D open to those who have completed A, B, and C.
Tuesday, Thursday, 10-12. Two hours.
                                     Professor YOUNG.

E—9 and 10. Students in D are offered an additional course of
reading on somewhat advanced topics, meeting *two
hours a week through the year*. The work has been based
on Ostwald's Outlines of General Chemistry.
Major work: A, B, and C.   Professor YOUNG.

COMPARATIVE PHILOLOGY.

A——A course upon the science of Language is given,
mainly by lectures, once a week. This is especially
recommended to advanced students of language and all
who intend to become teachers of language. A broad
survey is given of the field of philology and the history
of method. The general facts and problems connected
with linguistic development are discussed, and especial
treatment is made of the structure and evolution of the
classic and Germanic groups. For reference the follow·
ing are recommended: Whitney's Science of Language
and his article on Philology in the Encyclopædia Bri-
tannica; Strong, Logeman, and Wheeler's History of
Language; Henry's Comparative Grammar of English
and German; Brugmann's Grundriss; Sievers' Phonetik.
Given in alternate years. To be given in 1897-98.
Wednesday, 2. One hour.   Professor HATFIELD.

ELOCUTION.

A—1.   Russell's Manual of Elocution and Cumnock's Choice
Readings are used.
Section I., *Monday, Wednesday, 4.*
Section II., *Tuesday, Thursday, 4. Two hours.*
                                     Professor CUMNOCK.

B—3.　Study of the Masterpieces of English and American Eloquence (Burke and Webster, Erskine and Everett).

4.　Critical examination of the text of Shakespeare and vocal interpretation of the Tragedies of Lear, Hamlet, and Othello.
Section I., *Tuesday, Thursday, 8.*
Section II., *Wednesday, Friday, 8. Two hours.*

Professor CUMNOCK.

C—5.　Study of the Principles of Vocal Expression, in the reading of the best specimens of English prose and verse. Advanced training in Dramatic and Imaginative Literature. Instruction in creative Gestural Expression.
Monday, Friday, 9. Two hours.

Professor CUMNOCK.

D—7.　Bible, Hymn, and Liturgic Reading.
Monday, Friday, 11. Two hours.

Professor CUMNOCK.

THE ENGLISH LANGUAGE.

So many students, bearing certificates from reputable schools, and fairly well prepared in other subjects, have been found deficient in elementary English that it has become necessary to impose a test on all applicants for admission to any course in this department. This test covers spelling and the essential principles of capitalization and punctuation. Such a test will be given early in the fall term. Failure to pass such a test debars the student concerned from taking work in the department of the English Language till he shall have obtained a fair mastery of elementary English.

The following courses will be offered during the college year 1897-8—All are year courses:

A—1.　A Negative Course in Style. Four essays.

2.　A Course in Synonyms. Four essays.
Both required of all candidates for a degree.
Section I., *Monday, Wednesday, 8.*
Section II., *Tuesday, Thursday, 8.*
Section III., *Monday, Friday, 2. Two hours.*

Professor CLARK.

B—3.　A Course in Paragraphing.

4.　The Inductive Study of Prose Masterpieces.
Open to all who have completed Course A. Students are urgently advised to take Course A in English Literature before taking this course. Beginning with the Academic year of 1896–97, Courses B 4 and 5 will

be elective for all except candidates for the degree of
Bachelor of Letters.
Section I., *Tuesday, 10.*
Section II., *Thursday, 10.*
Section III., *Thursday, 11. Two hours.*

Professor CLARK.

C—5. A Course in Imagery and Versification.
6. The Inductive Study of Poetic Masterpieces.
Elective for all who have completed Course A.
Monday, 10, Thursday, 11. Two hours.

Professor CLARK.

D—7. Old English, or Anglo-Saxon.
8. Early and Middle English.
Elective for all who have completed Course A and at
least one course in German.
Wednesday, Friday, 10. Two hours. Professor CLARK.

E—9. A Course in Forensics.
Elective for all who have completed Course A, but the
number admitted is limited to fourteen. In case of an
excess of applications, the instructor reserves the right
to select according to the records made by the applicants
in Course A. A course in Logic (Philosophy A 3) is
required as a preliminary to this course.
Tuesday, 3. Two hours. Professor CLARK.

F—11. A Seminary in the Analysis of Style.
Hours to be arranged. Two hours. Professor CLARK.

G—13. A Course in Rhetorical Theory.
Elective for all who have had Course A, 1 and 2. *Two
hours.*

14. A Course in Condensation.
Elective for all who have had Course A, 1 and 2. *Two
hours. Tuesday and Thursday at 10.*

Professor CLARK.

*Major work: Courses A, B (given in 1898–99), C, either
D or E and either F (given in 1898–99) or G.*

ENGLISH LITERATURE.

A—1. The History of English Literature from Chaucer to
Dryden, 1328–1700. Robertson's History of English
Literature and selections from representative authors.

2. The History of English Literature from Pope to Tennyson, 1688–1892. Robertson's History of English Literature and selections from representative authors.
Monday, Wednesday, Friday, 9. Three hours.

Professor PEARSON·

B—3. The History of American Literature from 1607–1837.
Pattee's History of American Literature.

4. The History of American Literature from 1837–97.
Pattee's History of American Literature.
Given in alternate years. Omitted in 1897–98.
Tuesday, Thursday, 9. Two hours.

Professor PEARSON.

C—5. Bryant, Longfellow, Lowell.

6. Holmes, Whittier, Emerson.
Given in 1897–98 and in alternate years.
Tuesday, Thursday, 9. Two hours.

Professor PEARSON.

D—7. The Early English Drama. The Miracle and Morality
plays; interludes; early comedies and tragedies; the
immediate predecessors of Shakespeare.

8. Selected historical dramas, comedies, and tragedies of
Shakespeare.
Given in alternate years. Omitted in 1897–98.
Tuesday, Thursday, 11. Two hours.

Professor PEARSON.

E—9. Narrative and Epic Poetry. Folk-lore contrasted
with literary art. Ballads and the poetry of Scott.

10. Narrative and Epic Poetry. Paradise Lost.
Given in 1897–98 and in alternate years.
Tuesday, Thursday, 11. Two hours.

Professor PEARSON.

F—11. The Classic Poets. Pope and his contemporaries
and successors.

12. The Romantic Poets. Wordsworth, Coleridge, Byron,
and Shelley.
Given in 1897–98 and in alternate years.
Wednesday, Friday, 11. Two hours.

Professor PEARSON.

G—13. Tennyson.
  14. Browning.
        Given in alternate years. Omitted in 1897–98.
        Wednesday, Friday, 11. Two hours.
                                    Professor PEARSON.

H—15. The Essayists. Selected essays will be read from
        Bacon, Addison, Johnson, Lamb, and De Quincey.
  16. The Essayists. Selected essays will be read from
        Macaulay, Carlyle, Ruskin, Arnold, and Emerson.
        Tuesday, Thursday, 8. Two hours.
                                    Professor PEARSON.

I—17. Lectures on the History of English and American
        Literature. A weekly course running through the col-
        lege year. It is intended as a partial summary of the
        work of Courses A and B, and is required of all candidates
        for a degree except those who take Course A. A small
        amount of collateral reading will be required. Credit for
        this course will not be given if Course A is also taken.
        Monday, 3. One hour.   Professor PEARSON.

J—18. *The Modern Novel.* Lectures upon the methods and
        value of the different schools of fiction, with class read-
        ing, study and critiques of the work of recent writers.
        Blackmore, Stevenson, Meredith, Hardy, Howells, Gil-
        bert Parker, James Lane Allen and others.
        The Short Story. Its evolution and marked types.
        Readings and discussion of American short-story writers.
        Poe, Hawthorne, Henry James, Mary E. Wilkins, Stock-
        ton and others.
        Tuesday and Thursday, 10. Two hours.
                            Assistant Professor MILLER.

  19. *Recent Essayists.* Lectures on changes in scope and
        method of the essay since Bacon.
        Class study of nature and methods of literary culture.
        Hamilton W. Mabie's Essays on Books and Culture.
        Critiques and discussion of selected essays from Lowell,
        Woodrow Wilson, Professor Corson, Brander Matthews,
        Warner, Lang, Curtis and others.
        Modern critics and criticism.
        Some recent poets.
        Lectures with collateral reading.
        Tuesday aud Thursday, 10. Two hours.
                            Assistant Professor MILLER.
        Major work: Eleven year-hours, including either A or I.

K—20.   Seminary in English Literature. A critical study of some designated author, period, or subject. Open to graduates of this University who have made English Literature a major study, or to graduates of other colleges who have done an equivalent amount of work in English literature; and to undergraduates who have taken three courses in the department and are approved by the instructor. Those who take the course will be required to present a thesis embodying the results of their investigation and to pass a written examination. *Hours to be arranged. Three hours.*

Professor PEARSON.

FRENCH.

AA—1.   Grammar (Edgren). Reader (Whitney). Grandgent: Composition based on L'Abbé Constantin. Madame Thérèse (E. Chatrian).

2.   Moi (Labiche). Swiss Travel (Dumas). Mademoiselle de la Sieglière (Sandeau). Le Duc de Beaufort (Dumas). Composition and dictation. Designed for all students beginning French in college.
Section I., *daily, 8.*
Section IL, *daily, 11.*
Section III., *daily, 2. Each five hours.*

Miss FREEMAN.

A—   Modern Literature.

3.   Grandgent: Composition, Part III. Advanced Grammar. Reading. On rend l'Argent (Coppée). Tales from Coppée and Maupassant (Cameron). Contes de Daudet (Freeborn). La Chute (Hugo).
Grandgent: Composition, Parts IV and V. Reading. Places and Peoples (Luquiens). Prise de la Bastille (Michelet). Le Monde ou l'on s'Ennuie (Pailleron). Private reading: Histoire d'un Paysan.

4.   French Lyrics (Bowen). Le Pater (Coppée). Ruy Blas (Hugo). Le Mariage de Gerard (Theuriet). Private reading: Sans Famille (Malot). Dictations. Exercises on Idioms. Essays.
Ten lectures on Modern France (history and literature) in second term.
Open to all who have completed AA. Classical and

Philosophical students may elect this as a four-hour course, omitting the Composition. Scientific students may, in the third term, substitute for Lyrics and Drama a special course in scientific reading.

Section I., *daily*, *10*.

Section II., *daily*, *11*. *Five hours.*

Professor BAILLOT and Miss FREEMAN.

B—   Classic Literature.

5. Pylodet; Théâtre Classique; Le Cid, Polyeucte, Athalie. Private reading: Quatre-vingt-treize (Hugo). Grandgent's Composition, Parts IV and V.
Development of Comedy; five plays of Molière. Composition, Part VI.

6. Literature de la Renaissance (Aubert). Montaigne on Education. Classic Letters (Walter). Private reading, La Princesse de Clèves (Sledd). Original essays. Lectures. Collateral reading, with notes, from: *La Société Française au 17ième Siècle* (Crane); *Études sur les Classiques* (Merlet, Lintilhac); Jackson's *Old Paris;* Demogeot: *French Literature*; Albert: *Littérature Française au 17ième Siècle.*
Monday, Wednesday, Friday, 9. Three hours.

Professor BAILLOT.

C—   Literature of the 18th century.

7. Voltaire; Zaire, Mérope, Zadig, Charles XII de Suède, Montesquieu; Grandeur et Décadence des Romains. Lectures.
Rousseau, selections; Beaumarchais and Sedaine.

8. Mediæval Literature: Chanson de Roland, La Vie de St. Alexis (Gaston Paris); Extraits des Chroniquers du Moyenâge (Petit de Julleville). Private reading: Aucassin and Nicolette. La Fille de Roland (Bornier). Students are expected to translate from Old French to Modern. Lectures.
Courses C and D given in alternate years. Not given 1897–98.
Tuesday, Thursday, 9. Two hours.

Professor BAILLOT.

D—9.   Advanced course in Modern Literature. Eugénie Grandet and Contes de Balzac. Le Nabab (Daudet). Origines de la France Contemporaine (Taine). La Débacle (Zola) read privately. (Wells' Ed.)

10. Modern Drama. Representative works of Scribe, Labiche, Dumas, Augier, Dumas fils, Hugo, Coppée, De
Banville, etc. Class work and private reading with
critiques. Private reading from Pierre Loti (Pêcheur
d'Islande, etc.) and from Paul Bourget (Extraits Choisis).
With this course collateral reading with notes and ab-
stracts is required from the following works: Worm-
ley's *Balzac*. Pellissier: *Le Mouvement Littéraire du
19ième Siècle*. Brunetiere: *Le Roman Naturaliste*. Pari-
got: *Le Theatre d'Hier*. Weiss: *Le Theatre et les
Moeurs*. Le Maitre: *Les Contemporains*. Wells: *Modern
Literature*. Matthews: *French Dramatists*. James: *French
Poets and Novelists*. Saintsbury: *Essays on French Novelists*.
Tuesday, Thursday, 8. Two hours.

Professor BAILLOT.

E—11 French Seminary. The topics considered will be
closely related to those of Courses C and D; but students
will be expected to carry on special studies with prepared papers. For 1896–97 the assigned topics have been
The Romantic Movement, George Sand, Hugo as Dram-
atist, Daudet and Realism.
Wednesday, 10. Two hours credit. Professor BAILLOT.

F—12. Herdler's Scientific French. Articles from scientific
periodicals.
*Four hours (to scientific students only) to be substituted for
A—6.* Miss FREEMAN.

G—13. Conversation with privats reading. Open to students
who have had AA, but registration to be subject to approval of the head of the department.
Tuesday, Thursday, 2. Two hours. One hour credit.
Miss FREEMAN.

PRIMARILY FOR GRADUATES.

H—14. Graduate and Post-Major course. Clédat's Grammaire
du Vieux-Francais; Toynbèe's Specimens of French
Literature, Ninth to Fourteenth Centuries; Gaston
Paris' Littérature Français au Moyen-Age.
Hour to be arranged. One hour.

Professor BAILLOT.
Major work: B, C, D and E, or Italian or Spanish.

GEOLOGY.

A—1. Dynamical Geology. General discussion of the agencies now modifying the crust of the earth.
Structural Geology and Geography. Structure of the crust of the earth. Position of Strata, Cleavage, Formation of Mountains, Faults, Dikes, and Mineral Veins. Forms resulting from erosion. Instruction is given by prepared recitations, and lectures illustrated by lantern-slides, maps, models, museum specimens, and demonstrations in the field.

2. Historical Geology. Rock systems and formations are studied in historical order. Fossil plants and animals, characteristic of the larger geological divisions of time, are studied in their botanical and their zoölogical relations.
Monday, Wednesday, 10. Two hours, through the year.
Professor MARCY.

B— Advanced Course. In this Course topics omitted or slightly studied in Course A are taken up. Instruction is given by lectures, laboratory work with quizes and theses. Books in the Department Library, museum specimens, maps, charts, and photographs, are used by the student. Each student prepares a paper each term on the geology of some locality.

3. American Palæozoic and Mesozoic terranes. Characteristic fossils.
Tertiary and Pleistocene terranes. Glacial Geology.

4. Base-levels. Migration of Divides. History of Lakes and Rivers.
Tuesdays and Thursdays, 3 p. m. Two hours, through the year.
Professor MARCY.

C— Palæontology.

5. Palæozoic Life. Determinations and reference of fossils to systematic groups with reasons for the references.
Mesozoic Life. Determinations and descriptions of fossils.

6. Tertiary and Pleistocene (Quaternary) Life. Causes of geographical distribution of species. Origin of recent forms.
Monday and Fridays, 3 p. m. Two hours, through the year.
Professor MARCY.

D— Geological Journal Club.
Alternate Tuesdays, 4. One hour. Professor MARCY.
Major work: ten year-hours in Geology, Mineralogy and Petrology.

GERMAN.

AB—1.   Elementary course. Thomas's Practical German Grammar (begun), Harris's German Reader (begun), Stern's Studien und Plaudereien, first series (finished); Stern's Studien und Plaudereien, second series (begun).

2.   Harris's German Reader (finished), Thomas's German Grammar (finished), Moser's An der Majorsecke, Storm's Immensee, Stern's Studien und Plaudereien, second series (finished), Hatfield's Materials for German Prose Composition.

Section I., *Monday, Tuesday, Thursday, Friday, 8.*
Section II., *Monday, Tuesday, Thursday, Friday, 10.*
Section III., *Monday, Tuesday, Thursday, Friday, 2.*
Section IV., *Monday, Tuesday, Thursday, Friday, 4.*
Professor CURME (Section I.)
Assistant Professor COHN (Sections II., III., IV.)

A—3.   Bernhardt's Novelletten-Bibliothek, Vols. I. and II.; Ballads and Lyrics; Harris's German Composition; Hatfield's Materials for German Prose Composition.

4.   Two Classical Dramas; Ballads and Lyrics; Harris's German Composition; Hatfield's Materials for German Composition.

Section I., *Monday, Tuesday, Wednesday, Thursday, Friday, 10.*
Sections II and III., *Monday, Tuesday, Wednesday, Thursday, Friday, 11.*
Five hours.
          Professor Hatfield,
          Professor CURME,
          Assistant Professor COHN.

Course A makes a proper sequence to the preparatory work of those who offer elementary German for entrance, as well as to course AB. Classical and philosophical students may elect this as a four-hour course, omitting the weekly exercise in German Composition. This exercise occurs in four sections : on Tuesday at 8 and 11, on Friday at 9 and 11.

B—5.   Goethe's Life and Works, treated in the order of his literary development. Particular study will be made of the lyrics, Werther's Leiden, Wahrheit und Dichtung, Egmont, Iphigenie and Tasso. Open to those who have completed course A.

Section I., *Monday, Wednesday, Friday, 8.*
Section II., *Monday, Wednesday, Friday, 2.*
Three hours.

7. Schiller's Wallenstein-Trilogy.

8. Freytag, Der Rittmeister von Alt-Rosen, and Aus dem Jahrhundert des grossen Krieges.

Scheffel, Der Trompeter von Säkkingen, Lessing, Minna von Barnhelm.

This course covers the important historical periods of the Thirty Years' War and the time of Frederick the Great. A literary study is also made of Schiller, Lessing and Freytag. Open to those who have completed course A.

7 and 8 omitted in 1897-98.
Three hours.

Professor HATFIELD.

C—9. Poets of the War of Liberation. Lectures and Readings.

Wilhelm Müller, the Swabian School, Geibel, Herwegh, Freiligrath, and Gerok. Lectures and Readings.
Platen and Heine. Lectures and Readings.
The poets of the earlier part of the nineteenth century included in course C are studied with reference to the political and literary tendencies of their times. A large amount of illustrative literature in the Greenleaf Library furnishes material for assigned studies.
Omitted in 1896-97. To be given in 1897-98.
Monday, Friday, 3. Two hours. Professor HATFIELD.

D—11. German Literature of the Eighteenth Century, based upon König's *Abriss der Litteraturgeschichte.* The Greenleaf library is well supplied with materials for the careful study of every period, and certain texts will be gotten by all the members of the class.

12. German Literature of the Nineteenth Century. König's *Abriss* furnishes the outline, while the study of the best representative productions constitutes the main part of the work.
Omitted in 1897-98.
Monday, Friday, 3. Two hours. Professor HATFIELD.

E—13. Advanced group. The themes considered will be those described under course D, the distinction being made that the students enrolled under E will be engaged

in more special studies upon the points treated, with the
help of the abundant literature contained in the Greenleaf, the Newberry and the Chicago public libraries.
For this work one or two hours' credit will be given
according to the amount assigned. This course, which
is given on the seminary plan, is intended chiefly for
advanced and graduate students, and in all cases enrollment will be at the discretion of the instructor.
Friday, 4. One or two hours.   Professor HATFIELD.

F—15.   Rapid reading of standard prose works of Hauff, Ro-
quette, Scheffel, Freytag, C. F. Meyer, Auerbach,
Heyse, Stifter, Seidel and others, intended to give a
free command of modern prose.

16.   Historical German. Beresford-Webb's Historical German Reader, Schoenfeld's German Historical Prose,
Hoffmann's Historische Erzählungen. Open to those
who have completed course B, and to others by permission.
Tuesday, Thursday, 3.   Two hours.
                                    Assistant Professor COHN.

G—17.   Colloquial German, for practice in the spoken language. The subject-matter will be based upon Meiss-
ner's German Conversation, Fischer's Wildermuth's
Einsiedler, and German newspapers. Open to all who
have had one year's German, and to others by special
permission. The two hours of this course count as one
hour in term-credits.
Tuesday, Thursday, 9.   One hour.
                                    Assistant Professor COHN.

H—19.   Course in Scientific German, intended for those whose
major work is in the natural sciences, political economy,
mathematics, or sociology. Open to students who have
satisfactorily completed the elementary work in German. The aim of the course is to prepare students as
rapidly as possible to read the standard German works
and journals relating to their specialties. Gore's, Hodge's,
Day & Brandt's, and Dippold's Scientific Readers will
be used, and special assignments made to individual students with the co-operation of the heads of the scientific
departments.
Wednesday, Friday, 8.   Two hours.
                                    Assistant Professor COHN.

J.—21.   Recent developments in Dramatic Literature. The leading developments of the drama from the period of the Revolution of 1848 are studied with especial stress upon the more recent productions. The best representative works of the different literary movements are read and studied.
Hours to be arranged. Two hours.   Professor CURME.

K—23.   Advanced German Grammar, studied from a historical standpoint. The aim of the course is not only to familiarize the student with the leading facts of the language, but also to lead him to understand the forces at work in the growth and development of the language.
Hours to be arranged. Two hours.   Professor CURME.

L—25.   Gothic. Braune's *Gothische Grammatik* and Streitberg's *Urgermanische Grammatik*. The study of Gothic lies at the very base of the thorough study of all Germanic languages, and hence is fundamentally essential to all students who intend to study German or English historically.

26.   Old High German and Old Saxon. Braune's *Althochdeutsche* and *Althochdeutsches Lesebuch;* Gallée's *Altsächsische Grammatik* and Behaghel's *Héliand*.
Open to advanced and graduate students.
Hours to be arranged. Three hours.   Professor CURME.

M—27.   Phonology. Introduction to the Study of German Sounds and their History.
Hour to be arranged. One hour.   Professor CURME.
Major work: Courses B, C, or F, and D. After June, 1897, nine year-hours from courses other than AB or A.

GREEK.

A—1.   Lysias' Select Orations and Xenophon's Memorabilia of Socrates. Greek Composition based on the text.

2.   Lysias' Select Orations as a basis for Greek Composition. Homer's Odyssey.
Section II.   Same as above in inverse order.
Section I., *Monday, Tuesday, Wednesday, Thursday, Friday, 9.*
Section II., *Monday, Tuesday, Wednesday, Thursday, Friday, 11. Five hours.*
Professors BAIRD and SCOTT.

B—3.   Æschines against Ctesiphon and Sophocles, Antigone.
   4. Plato, Gorgias and Xenophon's Synposium.
Tuesday, Wednesday, Thursday, 10.   Three hours.

                              Professor BAIRD.

C—5.   Selections from Greek Lyric Poets, Æschylus, Prometheus Bound.
   6. Aristophanes, Clouds.
Euripides, Medea.
One hour per week is devoted to lectures on the history of Greek Poetry from Homer to Theocritus and to the study in translation of the masterpieces of representative poets.
Monday, Wednesday, Friday, 3.   Three hours.

                              Professor BAIRD.

D—7.   Demosthenes on the Crown.
Selections from Herodotus and Thucydides.
   8. Selections from Plato's Republic and Lucian's Dialogues.
One hour per week is devoted to lectures on the history of Greek Prose Literature and the study in translation of representative Prose authors from Herodotus to the Christian Fathers.
Monday, Wednesday, Friday, 3.   Three hours.
Courses C and D are open to all who have completed Course B. They are given in alternate years. Course D will not be given in 1897–98.

                              Professor BAIRD.

E—   Lectures on the Life of the Ancient Greeks.
   9   Greek Social life.
   10. Greek Religious life. Collateral reading will be assigned, and photographs, the stereopticon and collection of casts in the Art Institute of Chicago will be utilized for illustration. Open to students in all courses.
Two hours: To be arranged.

                              Professor BAIRD.

F—   History of Greek Art.
F—11. History of Architecture with special reference to the Greek temple and its influence on subsequent Architecture. History of Greek Sculpture to the age of Phidias.
   12. History of Greek Sculpture in the Age of Phidias and down to the Roman period.

As text books Statham's Architecture for General Readers and Gardner's Handbook of Greek Sculpture will be used.

The subject will be discussed in lectures and recitations, and will be illustrated by engravings and a large collection of photographs. The collection of casts in the Art Institute of Chicago will be utilized. Open to students in all Courses. *Two hours.*

Courses E and F are offered in alternate years. Course F will not be offered in 1897–98.

G 12 and 13.   Homer and Greek Epic Poetry.
A critical study of selected passages from the Iliad and Odyssey. Topics for investigation will be assigned, and papers prepared by the members will be discussed.
The critical work is to be supplemented by wide reading. Lectures will be given on subjects connected with the study of Greek Epic Poetry. *Three hours. Hours to be arranged.*
Course *G* is intended for graduates. Other students must give satisfactory evidence of ability to pursue their work with profit.   Assistant Professor SCOTT.

J—25 and 26.   The Synoptic Gospels and Acts.
Tuesday, Wednesday, Thursday, 11. Three hours.
Professor BRADLEY.
Major work: Courses A, B, C and D.

HEBREW.

Courses of study in the Hebrew Language and Literature are offered in Garrett Biblical Institute. Students in the College of Liberal Arts desiring to eléct Hebrew must receive from the committee on Registration a certificate of approval. Final arrangements are to be made with the instructor in charge.

A—1 and 2.   Elements of Hebrew.
Tuesday, Wednesday, Thursday, Friday, 9. Four hours.
Professor HORSWELL.

B—3 and 4.   Historical books.
Tuesday, Wednesday, Thursday, 11. Three hours.
Professor HORSWELL.

HISTORY.

A—   English History, with use of text-book.
   1. From early Britain to the Stuarts.
   2. From the Stuarts to contémporary times.
   Monday, Wednesday, Friday, 3. Three hours.
Professor SHEPPARD.

B— English Constitutional History, with use of text-book,
lectures, and writing of theses.

3. Anglo-Saxon Constitution; Norman Modification of the
Constitution; Growth under the Plantagenets; Early
Parliamentary Development; The Tudor and Stuart
Periods, and Modern Period of Reform.

4. History of Civilization: Ancient and Modern Compared;
Mediæval Development of Civilization; Civilization as
contributed to by European Nations.
Wednesday and Friday. Two hours.
Professor SHEPPARD.

C— American Colonial and Constitutional History.

5. Era of American Discovery and Exploration; Colonial
Experiments; the French and English in America;
The French and Indian War.

6. Constitutional Phases of Controversy between England
and the Colonies; the Revolutionary War; the Confed-
eration Period; Making of the Constitution; Its Amend-
ment, and Relation of the Supreme Court to its Interpretation.
Tuesday, Thursday, 11. Two hours.
Professor SHEPPARD.

D—1. Grecian History.

2. Roman History.
Monday, 8; Wednesday, 10. Mr. WILDE.

E— Continental Europe During the Middle Ages.
Text-books, lectures, topics.

9. Dissolution of the Roman Empire; Migrations of the
Germanic Nations; Influence of the Christian Church;
Foundation of the Mediæval Empire.

10. Struggle between the Empire and the Papacy; Cru-
sades.
Monday, Wednesday, Friday, 10. Three hours.
Professor JAMES.

F— Continental Europe from the Beginning of the Renaissance to the Outbreak of the French Revolution.
Methods the same as in Course E.

11. Inventions, Discoveries and Colonization; Progress of
Literature and Art during the Fourteenth and Fifteenth
Centuries; the Reformation; Period of the Emperor
Charles V; Revolt of the Netherlands.

12. The Huguenot Wars; Thirty years' War; Triumph of French Absolutism in the Reign of Louis XIV; Frederick the Great and Prussian Ascendency.
Monday, Wednesday, Friday, 11. Three hours.
Professor JAMES.

G— Continental Europe since the Outbreak of the French Revolution. Political History, showing the Progress of Democracy and aiming to give an understanding of the present condition of European politics.
Methods the same as in Course E.

13. The French Revolution and Napoleonic Period.

14. Successive changes in France after 1815; Unification of Germany and of Italy; the Eastern Question; Present Constitutions and Political conditions.
Monday, Wednesday, Friday, 9. Three hours.
PROFESSOR JAMES.

PRIMARILY FOR GRADUATES.

H—15. Seminary in European History. Open only to those whom the Professor in charge considers qualified. One meeting each week of one or two hours; but each student must give suffieient time to outside research to entitle him to three hours of credit. In case of graduates additional credit may be acquired if arranged for at the time of registration.
Hours to be arranged. Three hours.
Professor JAMES.

Major work, ten year-hours.

L— Post-Nicene Church History; History of the Reformation; History of the Modern Church.

31. Post-Nicene History of the Christian Church. Christianity within the Roman Empire; the Struggle of the Church with Paganism, with Barbarism, and with Mohammedanism; the Development of the Hierarchy; the Rivalries of the Patriarchates; the Upbuilding of the Papacy and the Growth of Monachism; the Relations of the Popes to the Byzantine, Frankish, and German Emperors; the Crusades; the Growth and Decay of Papal Power; the Monastic Schools; the Universities; the Mendicants and Mediæval Heretics; Scholasticism and Superstition; the Church and Mediæval Society.

32. History of the Reformation,—its extent, its character, its successes and failures, its causes and consequences. History of the Modern Church.
Tuesday, Wednesday, Thursday, 10.   Three hours.

Professor LITTLE.

ITALIAN.

A—1.   Grandgent's Grammar: Cuore (D'Amici).

2.   Montague: Modern Italian Readings (Prose); Manzoni; I Promessi Sposi.

Italian readings (Poetry); Selections from Dante (18 cantos); Private Reading; Alberto (D'Amici); Collateral reading required: Howell's *Italian Poets*, Symonds' *Introduction to Dante*, Church's *Dante*, Rossetti's *Dante and his Circle*. The courses in Italian and Spanish will be given in alternate years. The course in Italian is given in 1897–98.
Monday, Wednesday, Friday, 9.   Three hours.

Professor BAILLOT.

LATIN.

A—   Livy, books I., XXI and XXII.
Cicero, De Senectute and selected Letters.
(Advanced section).
Terence, two plays, Andria and Phornieo.
Latin composition and practice in reading at sight throughout the year.
Section I., 9 A. M. *Five hours.*
Section II., 10 A. M. *Five hours.*
Section III., 2 P. M. *Five hours.*

Dr. LONG.

B—   Horace, Odes, Satires and Epistles.
Tacitus, Agricola, Pliny's Letters.
Section I., *Tuesday, Wednesday, and Friday, 9.*
Section II., *Tuesday, Wednesday, and Friday, 11.*
Three hours.   Professor BONBRIGHT.

C—   Roman Comedy and Satires, selected readings and Lectures.
Historians of the Early Empire.
Monday, Thursday, and Friday, 10.   Three hours.

Professor BONBRIGHT.

D—   Lyric and Elegiac Poetry, selections from Catullus, Tibullus, and Propertius, lectures. Early Christian Hymns.
Lucretius, two or three books.

Persius; Seneca, selected readings.
Monday, Thursday, and Friday, 10. Three hours.
Professor BONBRIGHT.

Courses C and D given in alternate years. Course D in 1897-98.

E— Advanced reading under Course C, with study of assigned subject,—1896-97, the reign of Tiberius.

F— Schools of Philosophy at Rome,—Cicero, de Finibus, with study of other selections, lectures. Courses E and F, designed primarily for graduates, open to undergraduates on approval of the instructor. Given in alternate years. Course F given in 1897-98.
One or two hours. Time to be announced.
Professor BONBRIGHT.

G—15. Teachers' Course.—Topics in Latin Syntax, lectures and illustrative exercises; study of Preparatory Latin selections, with practice in class instruction.
One hour, in the last half year. Time to be announced.
Professor BONBRIGHT and Dr. LONG.
Major Work, B, C, and D.

LAW.

A—1. The Elements of the Common Law. Text-book and Lectures.
Monday, Friday, 3. Two hours.

2. Constitutional Law of the United States. Text-book and lectures.
The course will be given in 1897-98, and in alternate years.
Monday, Friday, 3. Two hours. The PRESIDENT.

B—4. The Elements of International Law. Text-book.
Monday, Friday, 3. Two hours.

5. Diplomacy and the History of Treaties. Lectures.
The course will be given in 1898-99, and in alternate years.
Monday, Friday, 3. Two hours. The PRESIDENT.

C—7. The Elements of Roman Law. Text-book.
Tuesday, Thursday, 11. Two hours. Second Semester.
Dr. LONG.

9. The Institutes of Gaius. Text-book.
The course will be given in alternate years, and in 1898-99.
Tuesday, Thursday, 11. Dr. LONG.

11. Administrative Law. For the Course in Administrative Law the student is referred to p. 59.

MATHEMATICS.

A—1.   Algebra. Text-book and exercises.

    2. Plane Trigonometry.
Section I., *Tuesday, Wednesday, Thursday, Friday, 8.*
Mr. KEPPEL.
Section II., *Monday, Tuesday, Wednesday, Thursday, 11.*
Mr. KEPPEL.
Section III., *Monday, Tuesday, Wednesday, Thursday, 2.*
Mr. KEPPEL.
Section IV., *Monday, Tuesday, Wednesday, Thursday, 3.*
Professor HOLGATE.
Four hours.

AB—3.   Algebra and Plane Trigonometry.

    4. Plane Analytical Geometry.
Section I., *Monday, Tuesday, Wednesday, Thursday, Friday, 10.* Professor WHITE.
Section II., *Monday, Tuesday, Wednesday, Thursday, Friday, 11.* Mr. KEPPEL.
Five hours.

B—5.   Plane Analytical Geometry.

    6. Differential and Integral Calculus.
Monday, Wednesday, Friday, 8. Professor WHITE.
Three hours.

BB—7.   Differential and Integral Calculus.
Monday, Wednesday, Friday, 9.
Three hours. Professor WHITE.

C—9.   Elementary Mechanics.
Monday, Wednesday, Friday, 9.   Three hours.
Professor HOLGATE.

D—11.   Determinants and Theory of Equations.
Tuesday, Thursday, 9.   Two hours.
Professor WHITE.

E—13.   Algebraic and Trigonometric Series.

    14. Solid Analytical Geometry.
Tuesday, Thursday, 8.   Two hours.
Professor HOLGATE.

F—15.   Geometrical applications of the Calculus.
Monday, Wednesday, Friday, 2.   Three hours.
Professor WHITE.

G—17.   Analytical Geometry. An advanced course.
Monday, Wednesday, Friday, 8.   Three hours.
Professor HOLGATE.

H—19.   Modern Synthetic Geometry.
Monday, Wednesday, Friday, 10. Three hours.
Professor HOLGATE.

J—21.   Integral Calculus. An advanced course.
22.   Differential Equations.
(Omitted in 1897–98.) *Three hours.*
Professor WHITE.

K—23.   Analytical Mechanics. An advanced course.
(Omitted in 1897–98.) *Two hours.*
Professor HOLGATE.

Major Work: Fifteen year-hours including, courses A or AB, and B or BB.

PRIMARILY FOR GRADUATES.

M—   Plane curves of Third Order, discussed principally by analytical methods; followed by geometrical introduction to Elliptic Functions. Lectures, with problems for review.
Monday, Wednesday, 3. Two hours.
Professor WHITE.

N—   The Theory of Numbers, Quadratic Forms.
Twice a week, first semester.
Functions of a Complex Variable.
Twice a week, second semester,
Hours to be arranged.   Professor HOLGATE.

MINERALOGY AND PETROLOGY.

A—   General Mineralogy, lectures and laboratory.

1.   A study of the shape, composition, color and other physical properties, the manner of formation and growth, and the use of minerals. The aim is to acquire ability to recognize common minerals and to gain a knowledge of the laws of the mineral kingdom.

2.   Blow-pipe analysis. Investigation and determination of minerals by wet and dry methods of analysis.
Lecture, Friday, 9; Laboratory hours can be chosen Tuesday, Wednesday, Thursday, Friday, 8-12. Three hours.
Professor CROOK.

B—   Petrology, lectures and laboratory.

3.   Optical characteristics and microscopic physiography of rock-forming minerals ; preparation of mineral sections.

4. Macroscopic and microscopic physiography of rocks; their growth and decay; their classification, etc. Open to those who have completed Course A.
Lecture, Monday, 11. Laboratory, Tuesday, Wednesday, Thursday, Friday, 8-12. Three hours. Professor CROOK.

C— Economic Geology.

5-6. The qualities, conditions, and surroundings of the useful metals in the earth; means employed in obtaining them; the quarrying of building stone; the mining of coal; the production of petroleum and related articles; methods of drainage and irrigation. These subjects are illustrated by maps and charts, pictures, and materials. Tarr's "Economic Geology."
Wednesday, 4. One hour. Professor CROOK.

D— Physical Crystallography.

7-8. Optical, thermal, magnetic, and molecular properties of crystals. Wooden and glass models, reflecting goniometer and microscope used.
Williams' "Elements of Crystallography "and Groth's "Physikalische Krystallographie."
Two hours. Hours to be chosen. Professor CROOK.

E— Field Geology.

9-10. Ice and water action, stratification, joints, fissures, occurrence of building stone and minerals of this region studied on short excursions to accessible points on several Saturdays in the fall and spring. Methods of field work and reports on observations made. Open to all taking other work in the Departments of Mineralogy and Geology.
Two hours. Professor CROOK.

F— Advanced course.

11-12. Special work in the investigation of rocks.
Three hours. Hours to be chosen. Professor CROOK.

G— Mineralogical Journal Club.
Alternate Tuesdays, 4. One hour.
Major Work, ten year-hours. Professor CROOK.

Courses C, F, and G are the only ones which are open to election at the beginning of the second semester.

MORAL AND SOCIAL PHILOSOPHY.

A—1. Ethics. Analysis of the phenomena of the moral consciousness. The theory of Ethics, with critical survey of the chief Ethical theories. Practical Ethics; the application of Ethical principles to the ordinary problems of life and of citizenship; the theory and the facts of moral progress.

There is no rigid recitation from text-books, the whole appeal being made to the student's reflective powers, as directed by the class-lectures. Still, certain portions of Muirhead's "Elements of Ethics" will have to be mastered. Students will be gradually given a complete bibliography of the subject, so that they may be fully introduced to it.

2. Sociology, Introductory—Theoretical Elementary Social Science and the principles of Sociology, the nature of the social problem and of social science; the conclusions of Anthropology and of the other sciences on which Sociology rests; the theory of Sociology by reference to the work of the leading social philosophers.
Monday, Tuesday, Thursday, 9.   Professor CALDWELL.
Three hours.

B—3.   Advanced Sociology. This course is designed to meet the wants of advanced students of the Moral and Economic and Philosophical Sciences. No student should think of registering for it without consulting the professor as to the desirability of doing so. The work done will vary somewhat from year to year. Three things will be kept in view: first, the Sociology of leading thinkers, ancient and modern (from Plato to Schäffle and Spencer); secondly, the more difficult questions in contemporary Sociology as represented by names like Spencer, Ward, Kidd, Giddings, Patten, Schäffle, De Greef, Gumplowicz, Höffding, Simmel, Tarde, and others; thirdly, the serious questions which arise out of the subject of Social reform. A reading knowledge of French and German, and work in Course C of Philosophy, or Courses A and C in Political Economy, would be most desirable in connection with the work of this course.

C—4.   Advanced Ethics. No student will be admitted to this course who has not attended A-1. In this course the history of Ethical Philosophy from the Greeks and Romans and Christianity to Kant and Comte and Spencer will be gone into in some detail ; also the present condition of Ethical Science, as represented by men like Spencer, Green, Martineau Alexander, Huxley,

Höffding; also the Science of Ethics as affected by Economics, by Biology, by Sociology; and lastly practical Ethics and Moral Pathology.   Professor CALDWELL. *Two hours.*

5. Sociology.   Practical application of Sociological principles to the chief social problems.   Immigration and Race Problems.   Social Pathology.   The conditions of dependency, or of the dependent classes — criminals, paupers, intemperates, the insane, and the weakminded. The modern state and its social functions.

6. Practical Ethics (Sociological). *Two hours.*   Professor CALDWELL.

D—7.   Seminary in Ethical Philosophy.
In the Seminary more advanced investigation may be made into ethical questions under the personal supervision of the professor.   Students will undertake special topics, such as Greek Ethics, English Ethics, German Ethics, the Ethics of Evolution, Political Ethics, and Social Ethics.   No one will be allowed to make special investigation who has not satisfied the professor as to general and special fitness.

8.   Seminary in Sociology.   The detailed study of some of the many different sides of Sociology may be entered upon, such as the Biological or the Anthropological, the Philosophical or the Theoretical (Social Psychology, Social Ethics, the Social Ideal), the Practical (the Administration of Relief and Charity, Penology, Social Reform). *Hours to be arranged.   Four hours.*
Professor CALDWELL.

Major work: ten year-hours, of which some portion may be taken in Political Economy and Philosophy.

MUSIC.

AA—1. Elementary.   Scale Construction and Intervals.   Harmonic sight-reading.

2. Harmonic sight-reading with Hymn Analysis. *Wednesday, 3.* (No credit.)   Professor LUTKIN.

A—   Harmony.

3. Intervals, Triads, Triad Harmonization with near Modulations, Triad Inversions with Dominant Sept-chord.

4. Harmonization continued: Addition of dominant and diminished Sept-chords with Inversions. Application of Cadence formulas.
Monday, Thursday, 2:00. Two hours.
Professor LUTKIN.

B— Harmony.

5. Secondary Sept-chords, remote Modulations, altered and extended Chords, passing and alternating Tones, Appogiaturas.

6. Suspensions and Organ Point, Harmonization of Chorales.
Tuesday, 2:00. One hour. Professor LUTKIN.

C— Musical Form and Analysis.

7. Composition of Melodies, Anglican Chants and Hymn-tunes, Song, Trio, and Rondo Forms, Variations, Inventions, and Suites.

8. Sonata Forms, Canon, and Fugue.
Tuesday, 3; Wednesday, 2. Two hours.
Professor LUTKIN.

D— Counterpoint.

9. Two and three part Counterpoint.

10. Four and Five part Counterpoint.
Friday, 11. One hour. Professor LUTKIN.

E—11. Double Counterpoint and Canon.

12. Fugue and Free Composition.
Hours to be arranged. Two hours. Professor LUTKIN.

F—13 and 14. Acoustics, Free Composition, and Instrumentation.
Hours to be arranged. Two hours. Professor LUTKIN.
Major Work: A, B, C D, and E.

NORWEGIAN–DANISH.

A—1. Modern Norwegian - Danish Grammar. Petersen's Norwegian Grammar and E. C. Otte's "How to Learn Danish," are the text-books used.

2. Readings from Andersen and Ibsen.
Hours to be arranged. Two hours. Dr. SIMONSEN.

PEDAGOGICS.

A—1.   History of Education. Lectures on Thursdays and
Recitations on Tuesdays and Fridays through the year.
Text-books: Compayré's History of Pedagogy, Quick's
Essays on Educational Reformers, Gill's Systems of
Education, Boone's Education in the United States.
Not given in 1897–98.
Tuesday, Thursday, Friday, 4. Three hours.

Professor FISK.

B—4.   Principles of Education. Lectures on Thursdays, and
Recitations on Tuesdays and Fridays through the year.
Text-books: Rooper's Apperception, De Garmo's Essen-
tials of Method, Laurie's Institutes of Education, Com-
payré's Lectures on Pedagogy, Lange's Apperception,
Herbart's Science of Education, Tompkins's Philosophy
of School Management.
Tuesday, Thursday, Friday, 4. Three hours.
Courses A and B are given in alternate years.

Professor FISK.

PHILOSOPHY.

A—1.   Logic. Ryland's Logic. Daily written exercises during the latter part of the semester.

2.   Psychology. James's Psychology (Briefer Course),
with class-room demonstrations and lectures.
Open to students who have completed thirty hours.
Monday, Wednesday, Friday, 2. Three hours.

Professor COE.

B—3.   The Philosophy of Religion. Lectures and required
reading.
Open to students who have completed sixty hours.
Monday, 4. One hour.   Professor COE.

C—5.   Elementary History of Philosophy. Weber's History
of Philosophy. Lectures, required reading, and dissertations.

6.   Locke, Berkeley, Hume and Kant. Lectures, required
reading and dissertations. Falckenberg's History of
Modern Philosophy.
Primarily for undergraduates who have completed
Course A.
Tuesday, Wednesday, Thursday, Friday, 8. Four hours.

Professor COE.

D—7. Theory of Knowledge and Metaphysics. Lectures, required reading and dissertations.
For graduates, and undergraduates who have completed Course A and have completed or are taking Course C.
Tuesday, Thursday, 9. Two hours. Professor COE.

PRIMARILY FOR GRADUATES.

F—11. Philosophical Seminary. Open only to those who have had the equivalent of Courses A and C.
Once a week for two hours. Professor COE.

Major work: Ten year-hours, of which one year-hour (or three term-hours) may be taken in Ethics.
For work in Ethics, see department of Moral and Social Philosophy.
For Collateral work in Greek and Roman Philosophy, see Greek B-4 and D-8, and Latin D.
For collateral work in Psychology, s e Zoölogy E.

PHYSICS.

A— General Physics. First year.

1. General Properties of Matter. Sound.
2. Heat, Electricity and Magnetism. Light.
Each week's work consists of two experimental lectures, one recitation, and one laboratory exercise. This course is recommended only to those who have a working knowledge of Algebra and Trigonometry.
Lectures on Tuesday, Wednesday, Thursday, 11: See below for Laboratory hours. Four hours.
Professor CREW.

B— Experimental Physics for students who have completed Course A, or equivalent.

3. Mechanics and Heat. An experimental study of Forces, Moments of Forces, Moments of Inertia, Elasticity, Heat measurements, etc., forming an introduction to advanced Physics.

4. Light. An experimental study of the general phenomena of Refraction, Reflection, Diffraction and Polarization.
Spectroscopy. Photographic and micrometric study of various spectra: application of principles of Diffraction and Interference.

Each week's work consists of two lectures and two laboratory exercises.

See below for Laboratory hours. Lecture hours to be arranged. Four hours.   Professor CREW.

C—   Experimental Physics for Second-Year Students.
5. Electricity and Magnetism.
6. Electric and Magnetic Measurements.
Each week's work consists of two lectures and two laboratory exercises. In the lectures, the most general phenomena and laws of electricity will be discussed; the practical equations employed in the laboratory will also be derived and discussed. S. P. Thompson's *Electricity and Magnetism* represents the ground covered. Course C may be elected only by those who have completed A.

See below for Laboratory hours; Lecture hours to be arranged. Four hours.

Professor CREW and Dr. SNYDER.
The Physical Laboratory will be open each afternoon in the week except on Saturday. Students may select their own afternoons for work; but having once made a selection this must be adhered to strictly throughout the entire semester.

D—   Problems in Physics.
7. Problems in Mechanics and Sound.
8. Problems in Heat, Light, Electricity and Magnetism.
Intended primarily for students taking Course A, and for mathematical students wishing to use their Geometry and Trigonometry.
Monday, 11.   Dr. SNYDER.

PRIMARILY FOR GRADUATES.

E—9   Graduate Course. During 1897–98, Czapski's *Geometrical Optics* and Helmholtz's *Electromagnetic Theory of Light* will be the subject of study.
Six hours.   Professor CREW.
Major work: twelve year-hours.

POLITICAL ECONOMY.

Those who wish to specialize in Political Economy should begin the work earlier than their third year in college; but no student will be admitted to any of the courses in the department except by special permission of the instructor, until he has completed the equivalent of one full year of college work.

In order to be admitted to any one of the courses, B, D or E students must have passed satisfactorily upon Course A or its equivalent.

They are advised to take Course F, also, as a preparation for these courses. *Course C requires no previous study of Political Economy.*

A—1.   Political Economy. An Elementary Course in the Theory of Political Economy. Recitations and Lectures with frequent written tests. Walker's Political Economy (Advanced Course) is used as a Text.

2.   Transportation. An Elementary Course in the Theory and History of Transportation. Hadley's Railroad Transportation is used as a guide.
Monday, Wednesday, Friday, 10. Three hours.
Professor GRAY.

B—3.   Administration. A Course in Administrative Law and the Comparative Theory and History of Administration of the Leading Modern Nations. The Course will treat of the general field of administrative study and the nature of Administrative Law, the Comparative Central Administration of the Leading Countries, together with a study of the legal relations existing between the different organs of Administration.

4.   Administration. A continuation of Course B—3. This Course will deal chiefly with the problem of local administration, and more especially with the administration of cities and their relation to the Central Government.
Courses B—3 and B—4 make a continuous course throughout the year. Neither one can be taken without the other.
Goodnow's Comparative Administrative Law is used as a guide for the lectures on Administration throughout the year.
Courses B and D are never given during the same year but alternate. Course B will be given in 1897–98.
Wednesday, Friday, 8. Two hours.
Professor GRAY

C—5.   Industrial History since 1750. Industrial History from 1750 to 1850. The effects of modern inventions and political changes on industrial methods and economic welfare. The formation of the *Zollverein*, the adoption of Free Trade by England and the discovery of gold in California and Australia.

6. Industrial History since 1850. The economic significance of the American Civil War, the Franco-Prussian War, the rapid extension of the means of transportation, and the tendency to concentration and combination of capital and labor.

Courses C—5 and C—6 make a continuous course throughout the year. Neither can be taken without the other. The work is conducted chiefly by lectures, with a moderate amount of written work. No text book is required, but topical references to the literature on the subject of each lecture are given.

Monday, Wednesday, Friday, 11. Three hours.

Professor GRAY.

D—7. Finance. A Course in Comparative Public Finance. General view of Public Finance. The objects and methods of public expenditure. Systems of taxation in the leading modern countries compared. The origin, methods and significance of public loans. The equilibrium of the budget.

Bastable's Public Finance is used as a guide.

8. Finance. A Course in Money and Banking. Discussion of the Theory, Value and Functions of Money, and consideration of the principal modern banking systems of the world.

Dunbar's Chapters on the Theory and History of Banking and portions of White's Money and Banking will be read and compared with other writers on the same subjects.

Second Semester. Wednesday, Friday, 8. Two hours.

Courses D—7 and D—8 must be taken as a single course throughout the year, and as such they are given in alternate years with B—3 and B—4.

Courses D—7 and D—8 will be omitted in 1897–98.

Professor GRAY.

E—9. Seminary. The seminary is open to graduates and to a limited number of undergraduates who seem to the instructor able to make original investigations.

Subjects can be definitely announced only after consultation with those who expect to take the work, the greatest liberty being allowed each student in choosing a subject for investigation.

Among the subjects suggested in the year 1897–98 are:—
"The Street Railway Systems of Chicago, their History
and Present Condition," and "The Office of Mayor in
the United States, considered Historically and Theoretically."

No one will be allowed to register for less than three
hours per week throughout the year in this course, and
no undergraduate will be allowed to register for more
than three year-hours, except by vote of the Faculty.

A room, containing a considerable library and tables
with a lock-drawer for each student, is set apart for the
exclusive use of the members of this seminary.

Tuesday, 2–4 (October 1 to May 1.)
Three to six hours for undergraduates.

Professor GRAY.

*Major work: Ten year-hours, of which three may be in the
department of Ethics and Social Philosophy.*

RELIGIONS.

A—2.   Comparative Religions.
Tuesday, 11 a. m.   One hour, second semester.
History of Christian Missions.
Monday, Tuesday, Wednesday, 5.   Three hours, first
semester.   Professor LITTLE.

For Philosophy of Religion, see Philosophy B.
For Bible Study, see courses under that heading.
For Greek New Testament, see under Greek.
For Hebrew Old Testament, see under Hebrew.
For History of the Christian Church, see under History.

SPANISH.

General elective, but especially adapted to advanced
students in French. The aim of the course will be the
acquisition of the power of intelligent reading. It is
expected that advanced students will make the same
progress as in the elementary year in French. The
courses in Italian and Spanish are given alternately.
Spanish will not be given in 1897–98.

A—1.   Grammar (Edgren); Spanish Readings (Knapp).
   2.   Readings, finished; Partir a Tiempo (Larra).
        El Final de Norma (P. de Alarcon).   Dona Perfecta
        (Galdos).
        Tuesday, Thursday, 9.   Two hours.

Professor BAILLOT.

SWEDISH.

A—1.   Modern Swedish Grammar, and the reading of prose selections. May's Swedish Grammar is the text-book used.

2.   Tegner's Frithjof's Saga and selections from Kuneberg.

Professor ERICSON.

ZOÖLOGY.

A—1.   General Biology. A comparative study of living organisms as a whole, forming an introduction to the study of vital activities. In the laboratory the student acquires a knowledge of methods of study, and is taught to observe, to verify and record his observations. A general survey of the properties of living matter is followed by study of a few selected types of invertebrate animals, beginning with the simplest and proceeding to the more complex. Parker's "Elementary Biology," and Marshall & Hurst's "Practical Zoölogy," are used as hand-books, and these are supplemented by lectures. In the lectures the physiological side receives most attention.

2.   Structure and Development of Animal Life. During the second semester a large part of the time is devoted to study of the development of animals, using eggs of fishes, amphibia and the chick. This course is open to all students, and is required of those intending to take either Botany or Zoölogy as a major subject. A knowledge of elementary physics and chemistry is very desirable for all students entering this or any of the following courses.

Lectures Tuesday and Thursday at 9 o'clock. Laboratory hours to be arranged between 9 and 12 Tuesday, Wednesday, Thursday, Friday. Four hours.

Professor LOCY and Mr. BIGELOW.

B—   Comparative Zoölogy. Two courses of lectures.

3.   Fishes, Batrachians, and Reptiles.

4.   Birds and Mammals.

Wednesday and Friday, 9. Two hours, through the year.

Professor MARCY.

C—   Cytology and Histology.

5.   Anatomy and physiology of the cell, microscopical structure of the elementary animal tissues, and principles and practice of the general methods of microscopical technique. Wilson's "The Cell in Development and Inheritance" forms the basis of the work on the cell.

6. Microscopical structure of.the animal organs, and principles and practice of the important special methods of microscopical technique. Piersol's " Histology " will be used as a text-book.
Lectures or recitations Wednesday at 2. Laboratory hours to be arranged. Three hours.   Mr. BIGELOW.

D—   Comparative Anatomy and Physiology of Vertebrates.

7. Study of Selected Vertebrate Types. The recitations and lectures will be based on Wiedersheim's "Comparative Anatomy of Vertebrates."

8. Physiology accompanied by Laboratory work. Walter's Physiology is used as a text–book.

[Note.—On alternate years, the work of the second semester will be on the Development of Animals instead of Physiology, as indicated above.]

Lectures, first semester, Wednesday and Friday at 9 o'clock. Laboratory work to be arranged on Tuesday, Wednesday, Thursday, and Friday, 9–12. In the second semester, when Physiology is given, there will be one more recitation period and one less Laboratory period. Four hours.
Professor LOCY and Mr. SWEEZEY.

E—   The Central Nervous System and its Terminal Organs. Lectures and demonstrations, adapted to those taking, or about to take, Psychology, and to others who wish to become acquainted with the structure and general physiology of the nervous system.

9. Comparative Structure of the Central Nervous System, with discussions on some of its physiological activities.

10. The Structure and Evolution of Sense-Organs. [Omitted in 1897].
Lecture, Tuesday, 4.   One hour, or accompanied with three hours' laboratory work.   Two hours.   Professor LOCY.

F—11.   Topics of Investigation. Open to students who have completed two years' work in Zoölogy. Problems of limited extent are assigned after consultation with the professor in charge, and worked out under his direction with such help as is required. This forms an introduction to the work of original research. The completion of the course involves the consultation of the literature bearing on the problem in hand, and the preparation of a thesis embodying the results of the investigation. A reading familiarity with French and German is essential for entering this course.
It may be elected as (a) Five hours or (b) Ten hours. Hours to be arranged with the instructor.   Professor LOCY.

G—13. Research work. For graduate students who have completed the equivalent of the courses described above. Similar to course F, but with broader scope and more rigid requirements as to the thesis, which must embody a critical review of the principal literature and substantial conclusions based upon the personal work of the student. Offered to students who are candidates for a graduate degree. Means of publication will be found for all papers which are worthy of it.

May be elected as (a) Ten hours or (b) Fifteen hours. Hours to be arranged with the instructor. Professor LOCY.

H—15. Zoölogical Journal Club. An organization of instructors and advanced students of the department for reports and discussions of biological literature.

Alternate Thursdays at 4. One hour.
Major work: Ten year-hours. Professor LOCY.

REGISTRATION.

The appointed registration days are the Tuesday and Wednesday preceding the first Monday of each semester. On the registration days of the first semester all students must register for the work of the whole year. On the registration days of the second semester all students must obtain from the Registrar certificates of registration. All matters of registration must be completed by the evening of the Thursday preceding the first Monday of each semester. A fee of $2.00 is charged for later registration. No credit will be given for work not regularly registered.

No one will be entered as candidate for a degree who has deficiencies in entrance work amounting to more than five hours a week through one year; and no student will be credited in the published lists of the catalogue with college work until these deficiencies are made up.

Required subjects take precedence in registration, in the order of their requirement.

Without special permission, no student may have at any time less than the equivalent of fifteen hours of work a week. Two hours of laboratory work will be credited as one hour.

Registration for more than fifteen hours is a privilege, subject to the approval of the Registration Committee, and it will not be granted unless it is clear that the student can carry his whole work creditably.

Entering students will be assigned to individual members of the faculty, whose advice they should seek concerning their college work, and such students are required to consult their advisers before they complete their registration.

ELECTIVES.

In making up his quota of time from elective work, the student may choose such courses as are open to him, subject to the regulations of each department; but having begun an elective year-course, he will be expected to continue it through the year, and may not change his registration without special permission.

At a date not later than the registration at the beginning of the third year, every candidate for the Bachelor's degree must elect at least one department in which to do *major work*. The specific courses constituting *major work* will be found mentioned under each department. They will involve from seven to fifteen year-hours given to work in the department, and distributed over at least two years of the general programme. The election of the department for *major work* will enter into the registration of the third year. The professor at the head of the department becomes the student's adviser, and must approve the student's registration in writing.

Students are urgently advised to give careful thought to the planning of their elective work as early as the beginning of the second year. They will find it much to their advantage to devote the whole or a large part of their elective time in the second year to the *major subject*. The faculty consider that the privileges of extended elective work will be made more profitable to the student by adhering consistently to his plan for the year, than by changing it, in the hope of improvement, after it is begun. The student is urged to consult freely with his adviser in all that relates to his college work.

MEDICAL STUDIES.

Students who contemplate the study of medicine after graduation are advised during their undergraduate course to elect the following subjects:

Physics,	Chemistry,
Zoölogy,	German,
Botany.	

Students registered in the College of Liberal Arts may elect studies in the Medical School of this University and have the same credited toward the one hundred and twenty semester-hours required for the Bachelor's degree. But in no case can more than twenty semester-hours be thus credited, neither can credit be thus granted for any subject for which the student has previously obtained credit in whole or in part in the College of Liberal Arts.

No time spent in the Medical School can be credited toward the year of residence in the College of Liberal Arts required of all candidates for the Bachelor's degree.

Credit for such studies is restricted to work done in the Medical School of this University.

Under the above provisions it is possible to obtain the Bachelor's degree and the degree in medicine in seven years.

LAW STUDIES.

Students who contemplate the study of law after graduation are advised during their undergraduate course to elect the following subjects:

Elementary Law,	Administrative Law,
Constitutional Law,	Roman Law,
International Law,	Diplomacy.

Students registered in the College of Liberal Arts may elect studies in the Law School of this University, and have the same credited toward the one hundred and twenty semester-hours required for the Bachelor's degree. The conditions under which this may be done are similar to those above stated respecting Medical studies.

Under those provisions it is possible to obtain the Bachelor's degree and the degree in law in six years.

The Law Faculty will give credit, toward the degree in law, for work done in the College of Liberal Arts in the law studies above designated, the credit not to exceed one year hour in any one subject.

THEOLOGICAL STUDIES.

Students who contemplate the study of theology after graduation are advised during their undergraduate course to make themselves proficient in Greek, Latin, and German. They are also advised to elect Philosophy, courses A and C, as well as Moral Philosophy, course A.

They are also advised that in the Theological Schools of this University they can shorten by one year the time required for the degree of Bachelor of Divinity by obtaining credit during their undergraduate course in the College of Liberal Arts in the following subjects: Hebrew, courses A and B; Greek, course J; and History, course L.

Full credit will be given for work done in the first semester, and for work done in the second semester the credit will be one and one half times the number of hours completed.

Credit in these courses cannot be counted toward the year of residence in the College of Liberal Arts required of all candidates for the Bachelor's degree.

ABSENCES.

When, in any semester, the number of his absences in a single subject exceeds one-eighth of the total number of required exercises in that subject, the student will be required to take, besides the regular examination, an additional examination in that subject on the last Tuesday of the semester. In the second semester this examination will be on the last Friday of the semester.

When a student's absences in any study amount to one sixth of the total requirement in that study, the student's registration in the subject will be cancelled, and the privilege of examination denied. This rule is administered by the Committee on Records and Registration, which has power to restore the cancelled registration.

EXAMINATIONS AND RECORDS.

At the close of each semester, examinations are held in the studies of the semester, but any student may be excluded from examinations whose daily work has not been satisfactorily done. A *supplementary* examination for those who have failed in the work of any preceding semester will be held in the forenoon of the opening day of each semester.

No student may take more than one supplementary examination for the same item of credit.

Incomplete work not made good before the close of the next succeeding semester shall be recorded as *failed*.

Students reported absent from regular examinations become subject to the rule concerning supplementary examinations. Those reported absent from a required *additional* examination are held to take that examination at the next date set for it, and no credit can be given until the examination is passed.

Undergraduates are not allowed credit for work done *in absentia*. Only those who have duly registered and regularly pursued their studies in their classes can be admitted to examinations.

CLASSIFICATION.

For the purpose of listing in the catalogue, the name of undergraduates are placed alphabetically in two groups under the headings: Candidates for the Bachelor's Degree, and Students not Candidates for a Degree. Opposite the name of each student in the first list is indicated the degree for which he is a candidate, and the number of semester-hours of work successfully accomplished. These lists will be prepared from the Registrar's records as they stand on the evening of April 15th, but names of students who may enter after that time, and before the publication of the catalogue, will be included.

DEGREES.

BACHELOR'S DEGREE.

The Bachelor's degree in Arts, in Philosophy, in Science, or in Letters, is conferred on those who complete the corresponding course of study.

On or before the last Saturday in May, each resident student who proposes to take the Bachelor's degree at the close of the next succeeding college year shall file with the Registrar a petition to be recognized as a candidate for the specific degree desired. This petition must be made upon blank forms provided by the University.

To be recommended for the Bachelor's degree, a student must have been in residence at least one college year, and must have to his credit at least one hundred and twenty semester-hours of college work; this must include all the work prescribed for the specified degree in the general programmes; it must also include the *major work* in at least one department.

Those who shall have to their credit not less than one hundred and four semester-hours, including all the subjects prescribed for their degree except Philosophy B, and who therefore need not more than sixteen semester-hours in order to complete all the requirements for graduation, may, with the approval of the Registration Committee, register their excess of time, above the one hundred and twenty hours, in work of some one of the professional schools; but the total work, collegiate and professional, shall not exceed twenty hours a week. The professional work shall be subject to any conditions made by the faculty of the school concerned.

Those who shall devote their excess of time to the continuation of their major subject, or to such other advanced topics as may be approved by the Registration Committee, may have such work, if satisfactorily completed, credited toward the master's degree.

GRADUATE WORK.

To graduate students courses are offered in advanced work leading to the Master's degree, and to the degree of Doctor of

Philosophy. All candidates, both resident and non-resident, before entering upon graduate work, and preliminary to the recognition of their candidacy, must make written application for enrollment to the Registrar, and furnish to him all data required for due record of their application. They must also obtain the written approval of the departments in which they propose to take work. This approval, with specification of the work to be done by the candidate, must be reported to the Registrar for record.

Graduates of this or other colleges, without becoming candidates for a degree, may, with the consent of the departments concerned, register as resident students in such advanced studies as they are found prepared to pursue.

MASTER'S DEGREE.

Graduates who have received from this University, or any other institution of accepted grade, the Bachelor's degree in Arts, Philosophy, Science, or Letters, may receive the corresponding Master's degree on the completion of approved courses of study equivalent in amount to thirty semester-hours.

Candidates who pursue this advanced study in residence at the University may receive the degree as early as one year after graduation. Those who do not pursue the study in residence may receive the degree not earlier than two years after graduation. A year of study in residence will be required of all candidates who have not received the Bachelor's degree from this University. The provision, "in residence," will require of all who are so enrolled an appointment for examination or conference as often as once a week with each of the instructors under whom their work is taken.

At least one half of the work offered for the Master's degree must be chosen from one or, at most, two departments of study in which the candidate has previously taken the undergraduate *major work*, or an equivalent. This advanced work will be known as the *primary subject*. The remainder of the work offered will be known as the *secondary subject*, and may be chosen from any department approved by the Faculty.

The Greenleaf Library, the gift of the late Luther L. Greenleaf, Esq., contains 11,246 volumes, also a large and valuable collection of unbound discussions and monographs, chiefly publications of foreign universities and learned societies. It is unusually complete in the Greek and Latin classics, every author being represented by the best editions from the earliest to a recent date. It contains also a choice selection of standard works in German and other modern languages. In the subjects of history, philosophy, theology, and the fine arts, there are many works of unique value.

The Orrington Lunt Library Fund, the gift of the gentleman whose name it bears, is set apart as an endowment for the purchase of books. The fund promises, as it becomes productive, to give the library large and permanent growth.

On payment of the regular term bills, every student is entitled to the privileges of the library.

During term-time the library hours are from 9 to 12 A. M. and from 1:30 to 5 P. M. In midwinter the afternoon time of closing is 5, except on Saturdays; throughout the year, on Saturdays, it is 4 o'clock.

The Library of the Garrett Biblical Institute, numbering 8,400 bound volumes, is at the service of students of the University. They have access also to the Evanston Public Library and to the great libraries of Chicago—the Chicago Public Library, the Newberry Library, the Crerar Library, and the Library of the Chicago Historical Society.

RELIGIOUS CULTURE.

The charter of the University provides that "no particular religious faith shall be required of those who become students of this institution." This University was not established with the view of forcing on the attention of students the creed of any particular church, but for the promotion of learning under Christian auspices, and to aid students in the formation of a manly Christian character. This continues to be its aim and purpose.

Students are expected to attend public worship on Sunday

in such church as they may prefer. A chapel service is held at noon of each day, and undergraduates who are not specially excused are required to be present at three fifths of the chapel exercises of each semester. The following regulations have been established by the Faculty respecting the observance of this requirement.

1. When a student's record of chapel attendance shows deficiency at the end of any semester, one semester-hour shall be added to the requirements for graduation of that student for every three credits needed to make good the deficiency. In applying this rule, a deficiency of only one or two credits shall be passed over to the next semester. In larger deficiencies, the excess above the highest multiple of three shall also be carried over.

2. When at the close of a semester the chapel record of a student shows a surplus of chapel credits, the surplus credits shall be applied to cancel any semester hours which may have been added to the requirements because of defective chapel record of any preceding semester; and the surplus chapel credits not needed to remove such semester-hours shall be transferred to the chapel record of the following semester.

3. When a student's chapel record shows a deficiency of credits for two distinct semesters which has not been removed by surplus credits in other semesters, he shall not be permitted to register again until permission is obtained from the Faculty through the Committee on Chapel by petition.

The Committee on Chapel consists of Professors Baird, Crook, and James.

Social religious meetings, conducted by the students, are held each week by the different classes.

A Young Men's Christian Association and a Young Women's Christian Association exist as distinct organizations, and exert a strong influence upon the religious life of the students.

A course of University sermons is given each year by representative preachers of the various evangelical churches.

The University preachers for the year 1896–97 were: the Rev. H. A. Cleveland, D.D., of Mankato, Minnesota; the Rev. George Elliott, D.D., of Philadelphia, Pennsylvania; the Rev. S. G. McPherson, D.D., of Chicago.

allowed to compete for any prize against whom, at the time for appointing contestants, unredeemed failures are recorded in more than one department of study.

The Kirk Prize in Oratory.—A prize of one hundred dollars, the gift of Mr. John B. Kirk, will be awarded each year to the member of the graduating class who excels in original oratory. The conditions on which the award will be made are as follows:

1. Five contestants will be appointed by the Faculty, and announcement of the appointments will be made the first Friday in May.

2. These appointments will be made on the basis of the rhetorical work done during the last three years of the undergraduate course—equal weight being given to the following records: (1) English A; (2) English B; (3) Elocution B; (4) Elocution C; (5) Orations of the fall and winter terms of the year of graduation; (6) The Oration of the spring term of the same year.

3. At this contest no prompting of the speakers will be allowed, and failure of memory will exclude a competitor from consideration in the assignment of the prize.

4. The award will be made by a committee appointed by the Faculty, but composed of persons who are not members of the Faculty. The decision will be announced at Commencement.

The Harris Prize in Political and Social Science.—A prize of one hundred dollars, the gift of Mr. Norman W. Harris, will be awarded to the writer of the best essay on an assigned topic in the department of Political and Social Science. For the year 1897–98 the subject will be "The Street Railway Systems of Chicago: their History and Present Condition." The conditions on which the prize will be awarded are stated below.

The Dewey Prize in Political and Social Science.—A prize of one hundred dollars, the gift of Mr. David B. Dewey, will be awarded to the writer of the best essay on an assigned topic in the department of Political and Social Science. The subject assigned for the year 1897–98 is: "The Office of Mayor in the United States, Considered Historically and Theoretically." The conditions on which the Harris and Dewey prizes will be awarded are as follows:

1. No undergraduate student will be allowed to compete for a prize in this department unless he shall have completed at the time of making the award the equivalent of courses A and C in Political Economy.

2. Essays offered in competition for either of these prizes must contain not less than 10,000 words, and must be either printed or typewritten. If typewritten, they must be on letter paper of a good quality, of the quarto size, with a margin of not less than one inch at the top, at the bottom, and on each side, so that they may be bound without injury to the writing. On the title page of each essay must be written an assumed name, and under cover with the essay must be sent a sealed letter containing the true name of the writer and superscribed with his assumed name.

3. The copies of all essays submitted for these prizes become the property of the college library, and any essay receiving a prize shall have indorsed upon it a certificate of that fact.

4. Each year the essays submitted for either of these prizes must be deposited with the Registrar of the Faculty before 12 o'clock noon on May 1st.

5. The Faculty will appoint three judges of the essays offered in competition for each prize, and the prize shall be awarded to the essay declared by two of the judges to be the best; *provided*, that the University expressly reserves the right to make no award of either one of these prizes in any year in which the best essay offered for that prize shall, in the opinion of a majority of the judges, not be of sufficient merit to deserve a prize.

The Gage Prize in Extemporaneous Speaking.—A prize of forty dollars, the gift of Mr. Lyman J. Gage, will be given to the student who excels in Extemporaneous Speaking.

1. At the first regular Faculty meeting of the calendar year the Faculty will appoint four contestants for the Gage Debate Prize, the choice being made on the basis of the work which those eligible shall then have done in the two departments of Elocution and the English Language.

2. To be eligible for this appointment a student (1) must be a candidate for a degree; (2) must have a credit of at least thirty-three semester-hours; (3) must have completed Elocution B and English Language A, and must have completed or be taking English Language B.

3. The debate will be held on the first Friday evening after the Easter recess.

4. The order in which the contestants, on either side, are to be called, shall be determined by lot, publicly drawn at the time of the

debate. Each competitor will be called twice, and will be allowed to speak ten minutes on the first call and the same length of time on the second.

The Cleveland Prize in Declamation.—Two prizes of fifty and twenty-five dollars, respectively, the gift of Mr. C. B. Cleveland, will be given to the students who shall excel in declamation.

1. Six candidates will be appointed by the Faculty, the selection being confined to students who have completed not less than 50 hours of college work, Elocution B included.

2. The announcement of the contestants for 1898 will be made on October 6, 1897, and the contest will occur on the evening of January 14, 1898.

3. In the competition for the first prize the declaimer's choice is not limited, but the second prize will be given only for a forensic address, poetic and dramatic selection being excluded. In no case may a declamation exceed fifteen minutes in its delivery.

4. At this contest no prompting of the speakers will be allowed, and a failure of memory will exclude a competitor from consideration in the assignment of the prize.

5. The award will be made by a committee appointed by the Faculty, but composed of persons who are not members of that body.

EXPENSES.

In Undergraduate Courses.—Undergraduate students pay, for the first semester, a tuition fee of $22.50 and an incidental fee of $12.00; and for the second semester the fees are the same in amount. The sons and daughters of ministers, as well as students who are preparing for the Christian ministry, and are properly recommended, pay $18.00 a semester, or $36.00 a year.

An additional fee of $2.00 is required of all students who do not complete their registration on the days appointed.

Students entering the College of Liberal Arts for the first time pay a matriculation fee of $5.00.

A diploma fee of $8.00 is paid by all students at graduation.

Students taking work in the zoölogical laboratory make a special deposit of $7.50 at the beginning of each semester, for materials, and for the use and breakage of apparatus.

Students pursuing work in the chemical laboratory pay the following laboratory fees: Chemistry A, $7.50 per term; Chemistry B, C, or D, $9.00 a term. Unexpended balances will be returned at the end of the year to students in both the chemical and zoölogical laboratories.

Students pursuing a single study pay a fee of $18.00 a term, except those who are preparing for the ministry, or who are the children of ministers, in which case the fee is $12.00 a term.

In Graduate Courses. — Resident students in advanced studies pay a fee of $15.00 a semester. Non-resident students pay a fee of $10.00 at the time of their registration, and on the presentation of their thesis preparatory to their final examination they pay a fee of $20.00.

Students whose undergraduate work was not pursued in this institution pay a matriculation fee of $5.00 at the time of registration.

A diploma fee of $10.00 is paid by resident and non-resident students alike.

Graduates in the professional schools, seeking the Master's degree under the provision stated on page 71, pay $10.00 for diploma. A matriculation fee of $5.00 is also required if the candidate's undergraduate work was not pursued in this institution.

Graduates taking work in the chemical or zoölogical laboratories make a deposit similar to that required of students in the undergraduate courses, and unexpended balances will be returned.

LIVING EXPENDITURES.

The following table exhibits the scale of annual expenditure in the undergraduate courses:

	Low.	Average.	Liberal.
Tuition and incidental fees	$69	$69	$69
Board (36 weeks)	90	135	162
Room	32	72	100
Washing	18	25	35
Text-books and stationery	10	18	35

Students living in Woman's Hall pay for room and board from $5.50 to $6.00 a week, according to the desirability of the room. Students in the College Cottage pay for room and board $50.00 the first semester, $49.00 the second semester. The figures given for Woman's Hall and the College Cottage include a furnished room, light, fuel, and the washing of twelve plain pieces. The occupants of the rooms furnish their own bed-clothing, pillows, and towels.

PAYMENT OF COLLEGE BILLS.

Payment of tuition and incidental fees will be required in advance at the beginning of each semester. Students who are unable to pay in advance must call on the Business Agent and state the case to him, and the President and Treasurer will, as a committee, consider and decide on the application.

No tuition or incidental fees will be refunded except in case of sickness. In this event, if the student will procure from the President an excuse from attendance, and also from a physician a certificate of inability to remain in attendance, half of the amount paid will be refunded, if application is made before the middle of the semester.

Students in Woman's Hall and those in the College Cottage pay their room and board bills one half in advance and the other half at the middle of the semester. No deduction is made for absence in any part of the term, except in cases of protracted illness.

LOAN FUNDS.

The University receives annually a considerable sum of money, to be loaned without interest to necessitous and deserving students who are preparing for the ministry, or for other forms of Christian work. Loans from this fund are available to students without distinction of sex.

A Woman's Loan Fund, contributed by interested friends and guarded with prudent restrictions, frequently enables the Woman's Educational Aid Association to be of special service to students in advanced classes, who, without timely aid, would be obliged to leave college before finishing a chosen course of study. The valuable assistance already rendered by the fund should commend it to friends of the University who may be able to increase it by donation or bequest. For further information on the subject, address Mrs. Joseph Cummings, Chairman Loan Fund Committee, No. 1838 Chicago avenue, Evanston.

SELF-SUPPORT OF STUDENTS.

Numerous inquiries are addressed to the authorities of the University by persons desirous of carrying on collegiate studies, but who are without adequate funds to enable them to defray their expenses, asking whether the institution furnishes to students means of employment which will enable them to support themselves wholly or in part while engaged in the prosecution of their studies. It is proper to say that the University does not undertake to furnish employment to any student, and it does not encourage students to matriculate who are entirely without resources. It happens each year that not a few students are able to aid themselves very materially by their labor while carrying on their studies, but the student is obliged to rely on his ability, industry, and character in all such cases. As the opportunities for employment are not offered by the University, they must be sought for by the students themselves.

For further information in regard to the College of Liberal Arts, address the President of the University, Evanston, Ill.

CPSIA information can be obtained
at www.ICGtesting.com
Printed in the USA
BVHW091739021118
531990BV00019B/982/P

9 781528 039833